THE NEW FIRE

Nick Francis

THE NEW FIRE

ISBN 978-1-912009-04-6
First Published by Compass-Publishing 2019
www.compass-publishing.com

Printed in the United Kingdom

A catalogue version of the book can be found at the British Library.

Designed and edited by The Book Refinery Ltd
www.thebookrefinery.com

Cover illustration by Andy Potts - www.andy-potts.com

For Antonia

CONTENTS

PART 1 - THE NEW FIRE - 33

Chapter 1 - The Communicator's Most Powerful Tool 35

Chapter 6 - Writing a Winning Brief 133

PREFACE

From the time humans first controlled fire, some 400,000 years ago, we've looked into flickering flames and been mesmerised. Fire creates a suggestive canvas where imagination, memory and possibility are given form. The ability to summon and harness fire is man's most valuable achievement. It provides light, safety and sustenance. Cooking our food has allowed us to break down more complex nutrients, making them more digestible. This gave us access to the energy to develop and enhance our brains. It enabled the consequent advances this has made possible.

Fire lengthened the day, allowing our minds to shift on to the non-immediate. Having completed the necessities of the day, hunter-gathers were free to spend time on more frivolous discussion. A study of one of the last such societies, the Ju/'hoansi bushmen of South Africa, found that topics for discussion changed significantly from day to night. While daytime conversation centred on necessity – foraging and hunting, and social dynamics – at night it turned to storytelling. Fire gave us the energy to grow our brains, and the additional time to use them abstractly – to think creatively and to forge narratives.[1] Through this, stories became the way humans shared information. It built on and defined the way the brain physically stores and recalls information. Thus, human knowledge and understanding is facilitated through our relationship with fire.

This perhaps helps to explain why our animal fascination with fire is without equal. Without equal, perhaps, until the invention of film. From the moment that Lumiere's train footage first terrified audiences in a small cinema in Paris in 1895, we've been transfixed by the transportation provided by the flickering lights of film. It's no surprise that, with the mass uptake of the television (TV) in the 1950s, the family's TV set supplanted fire as the main focus of family life (admittedly via the wireless radio). And there it stayed, through coronations, assassinations (from John F. Kennedy to J.R. Ewing) and space explorations. Only the Internet – the invention that is enabling video to come of age – has challenged, but not yet supplanted, its position as the epicentre in the modern home.

It took us nearly all of those 400,000 years to really capitalise on fire beyond its more basic form. It was another revolution, the Industrial Revolution, that allowed our relationship with fire to reach a new level. The work of many engineers, from Richard Trevithick and James Watt onwards, enclosed and harnessed fire, using it to create the steam engines whose use as a power source grew exponentially. They shrunk the world, and powered the manufacturing and adventure that started two centuries of Western-led global order. Through this evolution, fire became the conduit and facilitator, for the spread of ideas and power, which had hitherto been unimaginable.

Skip forward 250 years, and it's possible to draw parallels – on an admittedly more compressed timeline – between the democratisation of video and the profusion of steam engines that powered the new world order of the 19th and 20th centuries. The new availability of affordable video technology and the ability to share on the ubiquitous Internet have created a 'video explosion', beginning arguably with (but not initially driven by) the birth of YouTube in December 2005.

High-definition (HD) smartphones are the TV in our pockets. They are our portal to the world. Personal discourse is no longer limited to being in the pub, in the café or by the office coffee machine. Video is the most potent fodder for a social media infrastructure built on chatter, affirmation and sharing. It's the thoroughfare for the greatest flow of information in history. Like fire through the driest of grass, effective video spreads rapidly online, igniting interest and capturing audience's imagination. Videos that do this travel globally, while searing stories, messages and music onto our shared consciousness.

The power to create and share these videos is in the hands of the majority of humanity. Individuals have been made stars and millionaires. Some brands have forged a way, but business generally has not fully grasped the ramifications of the changes that have occurred. This book will help you to understand those changes. This book will empower you to harness the *New Fire*, powering your brand, your business, your people to new levels.

INTRODUCTION

Video Comes of Age

The breadth of change happening in the modern world can be illustrated by how crass it seems to start a book by talking about it. The last 10 years have seen ever-increasing political, financial and climactic challenges define the news agenda. We've seen an explosion in the use of smartphones: portals to a world of information and social contact. Planet-wide, instant communications promise to bring humanity closer than ever before. As data use has expanded, so compassion has been squeezed. The systems that idealistic pioneers believed would bring us together have given voice to undertones that are pushing us apart.

The Technological Revolution has allowed moving image to come of age. Millions of hours of video – the most emotive medium yet invented – are free at the point of use to anyone who owns a smartphone or computer, which is 2.51 billion people and counting, or just over 36% of the global population.[2] It can transport us, inform us, move us and capture our imagination, so it's no wonder that it accounts for nearly 80% of all online traffic.[3]

> Used properly, it's the most effective way to spread a message and build a following in the virtual world.

The power of narrative

In light of the bewilderment around us, people want security, definition and belonging. This drives us to seek out groups to align with and be part of – on social media, through sports teams or in businesses we believe in – to provide a little sanctuary as the world flashes by. These groups - all groups - are defined by their shared story: stories that help people to understand what the collective stands for, what is expected of its members and what they can expect in return. The clearer, more relevant and powerful the story, the stronger the bonds that hold that group together. Look at some of the most successful brand movements today, and you'll find the most compelling and effectively relayed stories: Apple – 'Think Different'; DeBeers – 'A Diamond is Forever'; and Nike – 'Just Do It'. These are brand taglines, but behind them lies a whole narrative architecture. Whether you feel drawn to them or not, it's difficult to deny their potency.

The power of any group – any brand – lies in the strength of its narrative. Everyone involved with a company is a custodian of its brand, both internally and externally. Those custodians must respect, nurture and strengthen that narrative wherever they can.

The 'Age of Transparency'

There are challenges with this, though. A reduction in deference for the 'establishment' has weakened the standing of traditional power structures – the police, the media, business, the government and others. These institutions used to put out a story – their story – and it carried weight because it was grounded in their own identity; their standing alone carried a degree of respectability or trust. There was far more scope for them to control the message for their own ends. This gave rise to public relations (PR): a whole industry devoted to putting the communicator's slant on events. But PR has had to evolve as the population has started questioning the basis of the established order.

This power shift is ushering in what has been described as the 'Age of Transparency'. Corporate spin nearly always finds a counterpoint in the hyper-mobilised online environment. The average consumer now sees 5,000 advertising messages per day – their minds are saturated and distrustful. In this new world, traditional marketing messaging is seen as being dishonest almost by its nature. The Internet didn't start this, but it has fuelled the fire. Now that almost anyone has the capability to share news instantly, any business that steps out of line runs the risk of their misdeeds being telegraphed to the wider world. 'Fake news' and (premature) belief that this is the dawn of the post-truth age make it harder for business communicators to engage and land their message than ever before.

Authenticity

So how should you respond to this? The winning formula is rooted in 'authenticity'. The buzzword-bingo-winning concept of doing what you'll say you'll do and being what you say you'll be. Being true to yourself and to your stakeholders, and not trying to be anything you're not. In the words of the vernacular, you've got to be 'real'.

A strange dichotomy is that our discourse has been infected by 'fake news' at a time when other people's daily realities around the world are more accessible than ever. The ubiquity of video production has played a key role in this. YouTube carries the breadth of human life experience, with a previously impossible depth. We can share in these experiences: a sinking inflatable full of migrants, a mountaintop wedding or the birth of triplets, with a simple search from our pocket-stored phones. No matter what the event, there is footage from every angle at our fingertips.

Traditional newscasting has struggled to define its role in the age of the omnipresent camera-/Twitter-wielding citizen journalist. News agencies' journalists are no longer the first on the scene. This has damaged the standing of news, fuelling an argument that it's in terminal decline. In spite of this, Vice News has grown rapidly – to the envy of an industry. It did this through more effective storytelling. Originally an alternative youth/skate magazine, it allows its contributors to get more involved in the story than news agencies have traditionally. By doing so, it tells the human story behind the news headline. The subjectivity of its reporting has led to accusations of Vice of being compromisingly partisan – of dishonesty with respect to the underlying news story. To this criticism, Vice founder, Shane Smith responded: "There is an element of dishonesty in a news reporter being shot at and not shouting: 'HOLY SHIT!'"[4]

This involvement makes the videos more compelling because it deepens the narrative richness of their news stories. One of video's greatest strengths is this ability to communicate emotion. Vice's approach injects human emotion, engaging the audience on a deeper level. You don't necessarily need to take the physical risks that frontline journalists do, but you must try to maximise the emotional engagement of your content (even if it's a training film) as this increases the impact and memorability of the stories. Portraying the genuine emotion of your subjects is a great way to do this. The key word there is genuine – your audience can sense artifice from the opening frame. You must find great stories and then tell them authentically. This book will show you how to do this.

The shift away from spin, towards more 'real' content can be seen in much of the communications shared by companies. Over the last decade, there has been a significant move away from the archetype of traditional corporate film: the big, glossy brand film. This was the type traditionally shown at company gatherings, careers fairs, the annual general meeting. These films followed most traditional advertising in tone, with relatively little nuance. Their message was effectively: "Look at how great our products and staff are, how happy our clients are, and how great we are generally."

This worked well in the unidirectional – business to customer/employee – world of Corporate Film v.1.0; keep 'banging the drum' and your usually captive audience would dance to your tune. Your audience are no longer captive; they can choose what they watch and when they watch it. They expect your communications to be nuanced: sharing aspiration and positivity, of course, but tempered with reality. The distrustful online environment means they view any corporation's idealised slant as at best detached and at worst actively dishonest. Neither of these are great outcomes. It is important to remember that anything that doesn't build or reinforce your brand has the effect of damaging it.

To overcome this, there has been a drive towards brand films that are more genuine in their portrayal of the commissioning company. For example: the 'ideal' sustainability/corporate social responsibility (CSR) film would be one where the company in question shares all of the good things that they're doing along with all of the bad. They are then effectively saying,

"We know this is not perfect, but these are the steps we're taking to be better." This treats the audience as informed adults. It leaves them to make a judgement, which is more inclusive of them, which in turn builds trust. This level of honesty can be hard to achieve – it probably sounds terrifying – but, for those who manage it, it offers an opportunity to positively influence the online discourse that accompanies their operations.

Taking this approach also means that it's not enough to talk about the good things you're doing; you actually need to do them. This means you need to act with more responsibility; it means you need to define and 'live' a clear and genuine business purpose. Simon Sinek's book *Start with Why*, is well worth a read in this area (you can check out his popular TED talk at www.newfirebook.com/links). In it, he makes the point that people don't buy from you because of what you do, but because of why you do it.[5] The idea of business having a purpose beyond the profit motive is well-trodden ground. It has many benefits, including more-engaged staff, better customer retention and a stronger bottom line.

A clearly defined purpose also gives you the perfect place to find the type of stories that will build your brand. This is because these stories tend to have a more pronounced human aspect by their nature. They are more relatable and memorable than much of the traditional subject matter for business films/communications. Because of this they represent an excellent way of humanising your brand and building trust with your audience. More engaging stories are more effective at achieving your objectives than less well told ones. Ultimately – as we will see - we need to maximise the impact of our content in order to maximise desired reaction among the target audience.

This isn't necessarily about spending more money either – it's about improving the subject matter of the stories you share. So many of the businesses that we work with miss out on potential returns from the content that they produce, because they aren't always willing to take more of a chance on doing something a little more eye-catching and special. One of the main reasons for writing this book is to try to get brands like yours to be bolder with the work that you do. It can seem scary, but with clear objectives, the right partners and the right approach, you can de-risk much of the process.

Defensive decision-making

"Fortune favours the bold."

– Virgil

The video distribution market is more accessible than ever before. This has made it more convoluted than it has ever been. This turmoil represents a fantastic opportunity for brands to make decisive moves and win fame and brand loyalty among a wide audience. To do that, to borrow a phrase, you have to 'think different'. By definition, to differentiate oneself requires a degree of unconventional thinking. Being conventional – producing average content – almost guarantees average outcomes. This is particularly true, for example, in the recruitment/talent space, where everyone in a given industry is chasing broadly the same candidates. If everyone goes about it in the same way, then the key differentiating factor becomes money. This makes it very expensive to get the top candidates. You need to try to break free from convention in order to differentiate yourself by what you stand for. The best way to illustrate this is through well-conceived, eye-catching video.

That's easy enough to say, I know. At my company, Casual Films, when we're asked for a treatment (the ideas and approach for a project) by a client, our creative team usually comes up with three suitable ideas. These are: a 'conventional but safe' example, a 'differentiating and could win awards/ really achieve something exciting' example, and another that falls in between the two. Even when the client starts the process by saying, "We want to do something really out there this time", the majority of the time (four times out of five) they go with the safe one. And, once it's commissioned, the client will tend to push towards safety as it goes. I don't mean this as criticism at all; it's more that I understand the pressures that commissioners are under. The people we work with are experienced, talented and creative, and want to create work that is genuinely great, but they often operate in a framework that doesn't allow them to do what they really want to.

The reason for this is that, in large corporations, it's nearly always better to be conventionally wrong than to take the risk to be unconventionally right. If you take a risk on the received convention – hiring IBM, as the saying goes – and it goes wrong, you're probably not going to get fired. If you take the unconventional route and it doesn't go to plan, you're out on your ear. This leads to defensive decision-making – the enemy of differentiation, and a factor that is probably costing your business millions in lost or unrealised revenue.

Learning from failure

The fact is that differentiation and, ultimately, success nearly always lie down the unconventional path. This is truer than ever in the content saturated world we're all operating in now. The way to allow your team or people to find that path is by giving them the space to take calculated risks with the material that they produce. I'm not suggesting that you completely let go of the reins and let the whole operation explode in a blaze of fruitless, but beautiful, creative glory. The key step in creating a winning culture is in how you approach failure. The businesses that really succeed are the ones that treat failure as a valuable chance to learn, and make sure that the lessons are heeded and shared across the organisation.

Matthew Syed talks about this in his excellent book *Black Box Thinking*.[6] He contrasts the incidence of accidents or failures in the airline and healthcare industries. Airlines carry millions of passengers all over the world in highly complex, heavier-than-air, metal boxes. On the face of it, this seems impossibly dangerous, and yet they manage the astonishing safety record of people having just a 1-in-11-million chance of being killed in a plane crash. Whereas, in the US alone, 250,000 people die as a result of medical negligence every year. That's the equivalent of three fully loaded jumbos crashing every two days.

The key difference between these two industries is their attitude to failure. In the airline industry, there are established systems for sharing even the smallest event from which future travel could be made safer. Pilots, engineers and operators around the world seize on any relevant information, implementing solutions immediately. In hospitals, people treat mistakes with a sad shrug and as 'one of those things' that happens when dealing with something so complex, yet, is it that much more complex than air travel? The key difference is in their mindsets: aviation has a 'growth' mindset – they are always open to improvements, whereas, regarding failure, medicine has a relatively closed or 'fixed' mindset.

You must cultivate an open culture where your team members feel empowered to try different things. You should encourage them to keep a growth mindset - always looking for ways to be better and improve. To use events that didn't go exactly to plan as an opportunity to learn. In the Silicon Valley vernacular, 'fail fast'. To avoid failing is to avoid the opportunity to learn and improve. The online environment gives you the opportunity to continually reiterate. It's more valuable to have the odd misfire, setting a baseline from which to improve, than it is to cruise along in safe, unremarkable mediocrity. Online, more than before, mediocrity is ignored.

Content is King

Content is king, but great content is the kingmaker. It's big business, and for those who get it right, it offers astounding returns. This is why, in the year to 2018, Netflix spent US$8 billion, HBO US$2 billion, and Apple and Facebook around US$1 billion each on content. They know that having the best content is their route to survival and success. But they are mostly media companies, so of course they spend eye-watering amounts on media, because that's what they do – it's their product. It's not yours though. Is it?

No matter what business you're in, you need to drastically change the way that you think about and produce video content. In the digital age, video is no longer just an element of your marketing. Such is the business value that a properly delivered content strategy can return for your brand, it's – bear with me here - more akin to an additional product line. Effective content is an essential addition to your value proposition. It's another channel that your customers/employees/shareholders expect you to use, whether you want to or not.

Your audience want you to share content that they value. There are a number of different ways to define value in that context. One way to think about it is that it's the type of content that your desired audience will seek out and would miss if it wasn't there. Marketing hasn't been about unidirectional sales messages for some time. It's about growing your standing by providing something of use to the audience. If you do it right, it gives you the ability to dramatically increase your audience's perception of your products or brand's value.

Brand value

At first glance, you might feel that chasing perceived value is little more than a vanity exercise. That misses the point. This is about improving your bottom line. It's impossible to make a distinction between the physical value provided by your products and the perceived value provided by your marketing. For example, it's impossible to make a distinction between the value generated for the guests of a restaurant by the chef (the physical quality of the food) or by the cleaner (the perceived value of cleanliness); i.e. it doesn't matter how good the food is if the toilets are backed up and the whole place stinks.[7] Video can be used to tangibly improve your product's value proposition and, through that, its saleability. This whole book is devoted to helping you to use this powerful, evolving tool to improve your bottom line.

Who's doing it well?

Energy drink company Red Bull is one of the most progressive brands in this space. It has pushed it so far that you could be forgiven for thinking that it has gone full circle and fallen down the rabbit hole. It runs its own TV channel, shares fresh pieces of content on its website and YouTube several times a day, and sponsors extreme-sports stars from every discipline going, even chess. The Red Bull Media House brand has a cachet among many of its target demographic that exceeds that of the original product brand. Red Bull is clear, though; all of this effort is about one thing – selling more cans of drink. Red Bull's purpose is helping people perform at their optimum, physically and mentally, so sponsoring some of the world's top sportspersons correlates. It helps its audience to see it as a brand that fulfils its aim, that it 'Gives You Wings'.

The endorsements these sponsorships provide are valuable in their own right, but it's the content that these give access to that hold the real value to Red Bull. It's the eye-catching videos that feature the sponsored sportspersons that really drive the brand in the online world. For example, its sponsorship of Felix Baumgartner's supersonic jump from space wouldn't have had the impact it had without Red Bull's ability to live-stream video to 8 million people around the world.

Red Bull's high-energy product naturally aligns with a high-octane, highly 'videogenic' take on the world. But there are plenty of examples of companies that have stepped outside the traditional marketing framework to establish a broader following online. General Electric's (GE's) use of its YouTube channel has been instrumental in driving the identity of the company as an innovative, progressive brand. Volvo Trucks has also built an influential followership with its use of different types of regular video on its channel. Throughout this book we will examine the opportunities that are available for other businesses to enhance their brand cachet through video content.

Brand Film Comes of Age

Video's coming of age offers progressive brands an excellent opportunity to engage with their stakeholders on a far deeper and more profitable level than before. This book will help you to see these opportunities and maximise on the return they offer. With Casual, I've spent over a decade helping scores of businesses like yours to use video to achieve their objectives. I've found corporate film to be a fascinating area, because it focuses on using the power of film to do so much more than simply entertaining or selling. It can be used to drive an almost limitless set of actions. Coupled with the breadth of channels that are now available to you and changes in attitudes to brand communications, you have an unprecedented opportunity to move people with your business messages.

That is great in itself, but there is a further opportunity. As we will see, your business now effectively controls its own content channel. You can choose what you show. What if you use that power to find positive causes and work with them and help them, at the same time as raising awareness of what your brand stands for? Successful pathways into this new way of marketing have been established. This is the best time ever to have the power that you do.

How to Use This Book

This book will give you a grounding in the value of video content for your business. It will explain why, what and how you should be thinking to maximise on the most significant technological advancement in business communications since the telephone, or arguably the printing press.

The book is split into two parts:

> » **Part 1** looks at the power of video as a communications tool and how advances in technology have put this power in all our hands. Now that brands have their own distribution channel, they need to think like traditional broadcasters. This means thinking about your content as an additional product rather than simply a branch of your marketing. It also examines the value of business purpose and the benefits of using it as a cornerstone for your content ideas/strategy.
>
> If you just want to get started, you'll find all the information you need in Part 2.
>
> » **Part 2** focuses on how to make video work for your organisation. It includes information on the production process, defining your audience, setting a budget and getting your projects seen by the right people. You may choose to use this for reference and dip in as you need it.

Why you should listen to me

Casual Films, or 'Casual', was one of the world's first digital-only production companies. We've produced nearly 10,000 videos for companies like yours over more than 12 years. I started Casual, with my university friend Barnaby

Cook, after working as a producer at BBC News. Our first commission was a series of 15 travel video blogs for Expedia in the summer of 2006. We produced these using just a camcorder and a laptop, and uploaded them from dial-up and early satellite Internet connections. That was before almost anyone had thought of the Internet as a medium for video, and most were barely the size of postage stamps. Even then, we realised that traditional methods of production were too clunky and expensive to service the vast potential for video the Internet had created.

From those early beginnings, we built a company that prides itself on the quality of its staff, its work and the satisfaction of its clients. Casual uses the latest production techniques, cutting-edge creativity and old-fashioned storytelling to deliver the most to its clients from this exceptional format.

I've written, produced and directed hundreds of films, and have won awards for creative quality and effectiveness all over the world. I've worked with and advised many brands – including Samsung, Nestlé and PwC – on how to get more from their content online. I'm telling you this because I want you to understand that I've been thinking about, reading about and researching the concepts in this book for over a decade, and I want you to trust what I have to say. In your hands is a massive opportunity, and not enough brands are capitalising on it.

Disambiguation

You may have already noticed that, throughout this book, I refer alternately to film, video and moving image. I've tried to be consistent in my use of these. Moving image is a catch-all term for all – ahem – images that move. One issue that I have with this description is that it misses out (in terms, anyway) on the audio element, which is extremely important in the overall impact of the output. Technically, a video is a piece of moving image (and probably audio) that is stored digitally (once upon a time this was on tapes such as VHS or Betamax). This means that all content shared online is technically video.

'Film' literally refers to the celluloid print that stored content before the advent of digital storage. Film production was naturally more considered and disciplined than digital production, because celluloid film is expensive and is consumed as it's 'shot' (i.e. as the images are captured). It's still used to this day on more high-end/creative applications. The word 'film' also came to refer to the output itself, particularly when it was of a higher quality, creatively and intellectually. Hence, 'Casual Films' sounds more edifying than 'Casual Videos'. The strange thing about the name Casual Films, though, is that, despite thousands of videos, we've technically never made a 'film'. I hope that clears things up.

Who should read this book?

I wrote this book to help senior executives to understand the how video works and how they can get more from it. I have found that there is often a bit of a knowledge gap between senior management and the more junior, but more informed/up to date, practitioners. This book addresses that gap.

That said, there is a lot in here that will benefit people working in every aspect of video production, marketing, human resources and communications. It will show anyone working in the sphere how video works, how to find and tell great stories and how to create plans that deliver results. It shows how video can be used to bring any business's brand story to life – engaging employees, attracting customers and keeping shareholders happy. This book demonstrates the value of business purpose in creating content that lands with your audience. It shows how you and your company can profit from the immense potential that results from using video effectively.

This book is designed to give a novice the knowledge and understanding that they need to be an informed, effective and successful content commissioner.

This book is NOT a step by step guide to hands on making films – how to hold a camera, set up an interview or cut a sequence for example. This is a book for professionals who want to commission a third party – a production company, internal agency or freelancer - to produce the physical content.

PART 1

THE NEW FIRE

CHAPTER 1

THE COMMUNICATOR'S MOST POWERFUL TOOL

"Marketing is no longer about the stuff that you make but about the stories you tell."

– Seth Godin

Video is everywhere. Cisco believes that video will account for 82% of all consumer Internet traffic globally by 2021.[1] The companies that have innovated with video have led a charge into a new sphere online, winning themselves valuations well into the billions. But (even if you're not a Netflix, YouTube or a Red Bull) there is still a huge amount that video can help you achieve. You may already know that but you might not know exactly what makes it such a powerful tool for corporate communicators. What is it in the qualities of video that make it 'work' for business? This chapter looks at the importance of brand storytelling, and shows why video is the best tool for doing it online.

As business communicators, we're interested in making the audience do something: to take a tangible, measurable action. That might be click on a link, buy a product or apply for a job. Whatever it is, we stand a better chance of achieving it if we can move the audience emotionally. As the old *Mad Men* era saying goes, "If you can make the cry, you can make them buy." To do this, we need to make sure that the video we share is as emotionally engaging as possible. There are a number of key elements that work together to maximise their impact. These are illustrated by the following equation:

Impact = emotional value of background story x storytelling x power of the medium (video)

We'll come on to the background story in Chapter 6. For now, it's what you are making the film about. The more engaging this is, the better the starting point you have on which to build the impact of your piece of communications. For example, a naturally moving charity story is a more compelling starting point than how to use a piece of software. Never fear, though, as there are still two other elements in that equation, with which to increase your audience engagement and, through that, the impact of the piece of video content. This chapter breaks down these two additional elements, and looks at why they work in the way that they do and why that's important to you.

Storytelling

Stories are all around us. We use them to entertain, to amuse and to inform. They also form the underpinnings of nations, companies, families, teams and even money. Storytelling has become a buzzword in corporate communications.

I HOPE THE STORIES YOU'RE ABLE TO FIND ARE A LITTLE MORE COMPELLING THAN THIS

A search of LinkedIn finds that nearly 800,000 people describe themselves as storytellers, or list storytelling as a skill. But there is good reason for this.

Stories are central to how we define our reality. They define belonging, and the concept of 'them' and 'us'. This is because every cultural arrangement relies (no matter how loosely) on a shared set of understandings. This makes an understanding of stories essential for those interested in creating and strengthening cultures of any kind.

What is a story?

Simply put, a story is an encapsulation of cause and effect. Our brains link facts – A leads to B, B leads to C, and so on. This gives rise to the three-act structure: the ingredients, the reaction and the outcome. The reason this is a more effective form of communication than just giving facts is that it mirrors how our brains have evolved to process information.

Story structure activates the brain in a way that simple facts do not. "Don't drink the water, it's not safe" isn't as memorable as "Sarah drank from that smelly stream, and she has been in bed, writhing in agony, ever since." When we hear the facts linked as a story, we can't help but visualise Sarah's experience. This creates an emotional reaction over and above the simple facts, and embeds it into our brains. Because of this, information relayed as a story is far more likely to be remembered than the same information shared as bare facts.

Good stories are about conflict; they include a degree of jeopardy in the achievement of the effect or outcome (i.e. A plus B could lead to C, but it could also lead to D, E or F). The greater this unpredictability or jeopardy, the more powerful the emotional connection, and therefore the greater the impact of the story.

This gives nearly all great stories a recognisable structure. Look at any of the great myths – ancient or modern – and you'll find the personable figure of the underdog, who sets out against great odds to achieve a significant (and almost unattainable) goal. In doing so, they enhance themselves and grow.[*;2]

In his excellent book Into the Woods, *renowned screenwriter John Yorke examines the mechanics behind story structure. He argues that, while the subject of the story (the protagonist) might not get what they initially wanted, they achieve the thing that they actually needed, and that is far more valuable.*

The reason for the success of this type of structure is that it mirrors an insecurity that lies at the heart of all human beings. Built within our psyches is the belief that we are the underdog facing the challenges of the world. Different types of stories resonate with different target audiences, but the underdog against the world resonates with us all. For more on finding and telling great stories, see Chapter 10.

Why do I keep talking about 'the story'?

Throughout this book, I refer to your 'story'. This refers to the narrative of the film – the process that you're bringing to life with video. This could include something that anyone would recognise as a traditional story – a 'girl meets boy' animation, for example – through to the structure that explains how to set up your new TV. Whatever your 'story', you should work with all the assets that you have available to clarify and strengthen the audience's understanding.

The 'Digitoral' Tradition

In the ancient, 'around the campfire' oral tradition, stories were alive in that they could be changed slightly and made more relevant for the listener each time they were retold. In theory, much of the 'dressing' could be changed, as long as the central truth, or moral, stayed the same. All stories have some form of moral, but most of these have only a passing relevance to a small number of people. The greatest stories, though, have a moral that is relevant to many people, as with the great myths mentioned previously. It's the ability to evolve while retaining an unchanging, central truth that allows stories to live and to survive.

This oral tradition survived until the invention of the printing press made storytelling a unidirectional process. The story, as printed, remained the same, no matter the audience. With the online world, the evolving nature of story is having a resurgence. Users take content and repurpose it, remix it or Photoshop it; each time making it relevant to themselves and their audience. Jonah Sachs calls this the 'digitoral tradition' in his book *Winning the Story Wars*.[3] It's up to businesses to create stories that are strong enough to encourage, while surviving this transformation.

Story and Memory

The paradox of the online world is that, while it has never been easier to reach an audience, it's still difficult to connect with them. There is so much noise in modern communications, but great stories give you the opportunity to reach past your audience's overstimulated heads and reach their hearts. Emotive stories do this. Used effectively, they enable you to get people to take note and remember what you want them to.

The facts that stories lace with emotional connections become far more memorable. In the early days of Casual, I used to go to breakfast networking groups, to meet and learn from other entrepreneurs. At one meeting, the topic of the conversation was, "What makes great customer service?" As we went around the table, the various business owners present gave their two-cents' worth: "Well, I think it's about sharing my mobile phone number and then not letting it ring more than twice when they call" and "I think it's about sending a card for your clients' birthdays". Each business owner took their turn to give their ideas. When it came to me, I had a story about something that had happened recently and was fresh in my mind.

"A good client of ours rang our office at 4pm on a Tuesday afternoon. They had a very important pitch, and, for one reason or another, the film that they had been waiting for from their internal video department hadn't come. She told me that the pitch started the next morning at 9am, and it would be severely compromised without the video. I told her not to worry and that if it was humanly possible, we would get it done. Four of us stayed and worked until 2.30am, finished the film and sent it over to her. She played it and they ended up winning the business. "This is what I think is good client service."

About a year later, I was at a conference and I introduced myself to one of the other delegates. I was slightly taken aback when he said, "I know you; you're the guys who are really good at client service." He had been at that networking group, and had heard the story I shared. It had stuck in his mind long after the associated facts of the rest of the group had faded. I'm telling you this to illustrate the enduring nature of information that has been made to resonate with a broader narrative.

Making the intangible tangible – brand, values and the 'foundation myth'

The previous example illustrates another key asset of stories in the business context: they allow the communicator to make relatively intangible ideas – such as customer service, brand or values – tangible. It can be challenging to communicate what is meant by an abstract brand slogan. If the communicator builds that definition out with a story, it gives it a form and context that is accessible and 'sticky' (or memorable). In this example, the relatively abstract concept of 'customer service' is given a clear form through a simple story.

Apple's iconic 'Think Different' slogan is perfectly encapsulated by Ridley Scott's equally iconic 1984 commercial for the launch of the original Mac computer (even though the slogan itself didn't feature for the company until 1997). The spot features hundreds of drone-like, monochrome men in boiler suits all captivated by a large, Big-Brother-esque face on a screen in front of them. From the back of the room, a young woman in running kit, including red shorts, runs in and hurls a large hammer at the screen, destroying it. It ends with a voiceover saying, "Find out why 1984 is not going to be like *1984*" – a clear, if implicit, punch at the established order represented by IBM. Anyone who saw that ad could see the essence of what Apple stood for then and what it continues to stand for now. To explain what was meant by the slogan could have taken many hundreds, if not thousands, of words, but video allows it to be captured and understood simply, in a handful of seconds.

This attribute makes the format really useful for internal/employer communications. Every company now has a set of values, which it expects its staff to live their working lives by. These values are far more effectively communicated through a story than a slogan. A value with a story becomes a behaviour. A behaviour is easier for the employee to understand and act on. Saying, "This is what we mean by excellent customer service, integrity, give more, etc." is a great way to get staff to exhibit those values. Video is an effective way of illustrating these stories to them.

The powerfully aligning nature of narrative is part of the reason that foundation myths hold such a powerful sway in the business world. Yes, the company may now be a global behemoth, but, once upon a time, it was just a small group of people with an idea and a desire to go against the system. These founders faced almost impossible odds (conflict/jeopardy), but overcame them with guile and a belief that what they were doing was right. No matter how large and successful the company becomes, there will always be the underlying narrative, which can be mythologised, and used to engage and motivate staff and other stakeholders.

Stories and belonging

Before each hunt, some Native American Navajo tribes would consult a shaman, seeking blessing from the spirit world for their forthcoming foray. He would take the hip bone of a bison and carve a few symbols into its surface. Incantations would be chanted, and the bone thrown into the fire. The hunters would gather round as the flames licked over its surface. Before long, the heat would crack the bone. The angle of the crack was seen as the direction for the hunt that had been blessed by the spirit world. Pleased that they were thereby aligned with the wishes of higher powers, the hunters would pick up their bows and arrows, and head off across the plain in search of their quarry.

To rational, secular eyes, there are a couple of elements at work here. Firstly, the crack would send them off in a randomly generated direction each time, meaning that they never overhunted any particular area. But, secondly, and more importantly, it provided the hunting group with one agreed direction that they were going to go hunting in. It meant that they started off in a direction that had been ordained by an unquestionable power. Without this aligning force, the group ran the risk of members griping and sowing further division when things didn't go to plan. The 'divine crack compass' was a story that all the hunters bought into. It bonded the hunting group, and ensured that, whatever the outcome of the hunt, the hunters would stay as a unit. This significantly increased the long-term prospects of the group.*

Why this matters to you

Having a shared understanding of a central story thus allowed the hunters to achieve their aims. As we've seen, we all use stories in our lives and in business, whether we're engaging an audience in a presentation, inducting a new joiner on their first day or telling a child where babies come from. It's useful to think of your company's brand as a narrative that helps your key stakeholders to understand their relationship with the wider enterprise. The more clearly and evocatively you can communicate that story, the more chance you have of the audience taking the action that you desire. That could be additional sales from customers, more discretionary effort from employees or better trust in the company's direction among shareholders.

Internal vs external brand

Although there used to be a clear distinction between your three key stakeholder groups (employees, customers and shareholders), which allowed businesses to communicate to them separately, the majority of your brand messaging can now be found online by anyone.

---

* Over the years, Casual has become a specialist in employer communications and branding video production. In a sense, this field is the modern business take on the hunters gathering around the cracking bison bones. It's about defining and promoting the shared narrative that binds the staff of any given company together. Albeit not in a random 'let's throw it in the fire and see where the crack sends us' way – not usually anyway!

Although the concepts that it draws on are as old as business itself, employer branding is actually a relatively new discipline (only occurring in the last 10–15 years or so). It's based on the idea that staff are the face of the brand in the customer's eyes. Because of this, it's important that they 'live the brand'; i.e. that they have a clear understanding what is expected of them, how they should behave and what they should expect in return. Stories about the company are a key tool in helping with this alignment.

This has led to a significant blurring of the line between the external and internal brand. This makes it even more important for business communicators to look for stories to share that engage and work for all three groups. The groups interlock for two reasons. Firstly, individuals may see communications meant for other groups. Secondly, they may belong to more than one group. Employees may be customers or even stockholders, and vice versa. Because of this, you need to try to find stories that resonate with each group's motivations. The perfect corporate film exists at the intersection between the interests of the three groups, as shown in the following diagram:

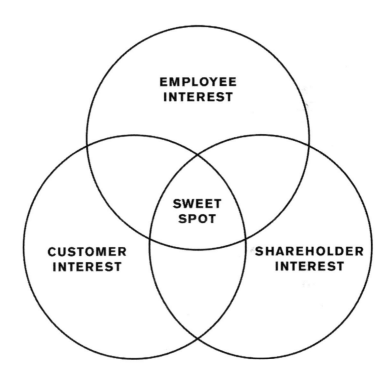

Figure 1. The stakeholder sweet spot

The Emotive Power of Video

Sergei Eisenstein, 1925 – genius filmmaker of the Russian Revolution

"Of all the arts the most important for us is the cinema."

– Vladimir Lenin

The leaders of the Russian Revolution were fascinated with the power of film as a propaganda and educational tool for a largely illiterate population. The reason for this is the medium's ability to inspire emotion among groups of people. One hundred years on, film/video remains the most potent tool available for generating emotion in any target audience. It's the ability to move us that makes good cinema completely spellbinding, and why, historically, TV advertising has been so lucrative. We are moved because we empathise directly with what happens to the characters on screen.

We've seen that storytelling is an essential tool in any corporate communicator's arsenal, for all the reasons covered previously. It's when it's combined with the natural properties of film that it becomes the most powerful communication tool available to humanity. This is because video is most effective when used to portray emotion. In this section, we're going to spend a bit of time looking at why this is and why that matters to you.

"They may forget what you said – but they will never forget how you made them feel."
– Carl W. Buehner

What is empathy?

empathy

ˈɛmpəθi/

noun

"The ability to understand and share the feelings of another."[4]

Empathy is a key evolutionary skill. It's fundamental to our ability to form cohesive social groups. It allowed our forebears to benefit from not having to fight sabre-toothed tigers literally alone. It allows us the same benefit, metaphorically speaking. When we see or hear about people experiencing emotions, we've evolved to feel those same emotions. For example, if we see someone who's suffering from the cold, we feel a little of that suffering. This makes us more likely to offer a jacket, blanket or space by the fire. These emotions assist the survival of the species, and are part of our basic need to seek out experiences, understanding and companionship. These are fundamental elements in what makes us human.

Why does this happen?

The mechanics behind empathy have historically baffled neuroscientists. To begin with, it was assumed that the emotion was as a result of a logical, mental interpretation in order to predict other people's actions. Then, in the early 1990s, Italian researchers studying the brains of macaque monkeys made a breakthrough. They discovered that the same area of the brain lights up in monkeys that are just watching their fellow monkeys reaching for food as in those who are doing the reaching.

This led to the discovery in the brain of what are called 'mirror cells'. This profoundly changed our understanding of neurochemistry. These cells allow us to understand other people's actions, not by thinking through what they are doing but by directly feeling the emotion that they are feeling. When you see someone frown, for example, your frowning mirror neurons fire up too, creating the sensation in your own mind that you associate with frowning. You don't have to experience what the other person is experiencing to make them frown; you feel the emotion directly and effortlessly.

Professor Talma Hendler, a neuroscientist at Tel Aviv University in Israel, studied brain scans in order to understand the chemical basis for empathy.[5] She found there are two types of empathy at work, which are illustrated by where they occur in the brain. The first and more advanced type is what she calls 'mental empathy'. This requires the viewers to think outside themselves – to mentally put themselves in the other person's shoes – and think about what they may be experiencing. The second is called 'embodied empathy'. This is a more intuitive and primal empathy, which you might experience when watching someone get hurt.

As part of her studies, Prof. Hendler showed Aron Aronofsky's film *Black Swan* to a number of subjects, while monitoring their brain activity. This intense psychological thriller (which I watched on a very bumpy flight in what was the most potently dramatic cinema experience of my entire life) actually made the same parts of the brain light up as those in the brains of actual sufferers of schizophrenia. As Natalie Portman's character experiences hallucinations at the depths of her psychosis, the audience develops – temporarily – the same brain chemistry as a genuine schizophrenia sufferer. Watching a film of someone with a psychological illness effectively gives the audience the symptoms of a psychological illness.

This makes film an invaluable tool for marketers. What better way of illustrating the refreshing nature of your beer than by transporting your audience to a hot desert and then showing some bottles sticking out of an ice bucket, complete with condensation? The advertisers are generating the perception of genuine thirst and potential refreshment for the audience. This fact explains the continued success of video advertising.

Anthropomorphic empathy

A strange quirk of this empathy is that we have a tendency to project our own emotions, motives and thoughts back onto the characters that we're watching. It doesn't even need to be a real person in order to elicit this effect. In order to empathise with a character, we just need to be able to attribute human emotions and objectives to them. Once this has taken place, we immediately and unconsciously decide whether we a) like them, and b) can trust them. It's this peculiarity that allows cartoons and animations to work.

Whether we're looking at a duck, a stick or a collection of pencil lines on the screen that make up a cartoon character, the effect is the same. We do find it easier if the item has a semblance of a face. The more like us the characters are, the easier we find it to empathise with them. The concept and ridiculousness of this is brilliantly illustrated in Spike Jonze's 'The Lamp' advert for IKEA.*;[6]

There are other things that a filmmaker can do to increase the amount we empathise with a subject. For example, we're biologically programmed to empathise more with children or those with childlike characteristics. Characters that are small, have big eyes or have a cuddliness to them (i.e. that are cute) are more easily relatable. We naturally feel more is at stake in their survival and so care more about their concerns. This is our base programming at work – our genes working to ensure their own survival. Music also has the effect of increasing the level of empathy with characters that viewers feel, because it adds to the illusion of their own vitality and personality.

The Importance of Aesthetics – Film Grammar

In order for this empathetic effect to work, the film needs to be convincing enough to trick the brain into suspending disbelief. It needs to 'work'. You may have noticed that there tends to be a consensus on the way films should be put together. You can watch a piece of film content, and make

---

Go to www.newfirebook.com/links to see the film

a judgement that it either works or doesn't. This isn't to say that everyone always agrees, but it's possible to look at a piece of work and decide whether you 'buy' the way the message it carries is sold to you, the audience. Films that follow this process of 'working' adhere to an unwritten set of rules known as 'film grammar'. Simply put, film grammar refers to the usage of all the different elements that go together to create the effect of watching the film back. These include camera techniques, editing techniques, and the manipulation of time, sound, lighting, graphics and the style in which the whole production is drawn together.

Film grammar was established in the early days of the 20th century, when pioneers such as D.W. Griffith used the new medium to tell stories for the first time. These early filmmakers used different angles, camera lenses and edits to illustrate the narrative that they were trying to portray. For example, one of their many discoveries is that when two unrelated shots are shown, one after the other, the brain automatically sees a connection between them.

If we see a small baby on a mat, followed by a large tiger walking through a garden, we presume that the baby must be in danger. This is even though they may have nothing to do with each other beyond being shown one after the other. The filmmakers then used this quirk of our perception to build a sense of tension for the audience. Through gradually experimenting with a number of different techniques, they established a language that remains true today.

Suspension of disbelief

Despite the fact that the viewer knows that they are watching a creative construct, the primitive functions of the brain are involuntarily filling in the gaps. This creates the same effect as if the portrayed events are happening for real in front of them. The filmmaker has managed to transport the brains of the audience to a reality of the filmmaker's imagination. Of course, the viewer knows that what they are watching has been put together intentionally, but it must be done in such a way that it allows them to suspend their disbelief.

The combination of elements can be changed to give a different effect for the viewer, but this needs to be done without breaking the illusion. Every element within the film has the potential to either add or detract from the illusion of the imagined reality. As a filmmaker, it's important that every element of the production – from the script to the hair styles to the edit – work together to serve the narrative that you're communicating.

For example, in the 'found footage' horror film *The Blair Witch Project*, it's important that all the material is filmed in a way that could have been achieved with a handicam. If they had edited in a perfectly smooth crane shot, it would have contradicted the key concept that it was all shot by the subjects themselves. These rules can be creatively interpreted in endless different ways. Interesting and effectively used grammar is the most powerful tool in the filmmaker's arsenal.

Grammar online

Like any art form, once you understand the rules, it's possible to look at ways of 'bending' them. One of the great evolutions in recent years is that audiences have become so much more aware of the process behind film construction. This means that grammar in online film can be more liberally applied. The 'jump cut' is one of the clearest examples of this.

Back in the old days of the 20th century, filmmakers took great pride in creating films that were as seamless as possible. This led to what is known as the cut away, where background footage would be used to cover the cuts in dialogue. In more hastily produced online films, where editors are cutting pieces to camera without the benefit of a large amount of cutaway material, jump cuts have become a more accepted editing technique. It has now been incorporated into film grammar, adding a 'poppy' air of immediacy.

The way a film is made says a lot to your audience about the body that made it. In the traditional, unidirectional model of corporate communications, it was important for businesses to put out a polished façade in everything they shared. This has changed in the drive for businesses to be seen as more human and authentic.

In Summary: The Communicator's Most Powerful Tool

In this chapter, we've looked at the factors that make video such an effective tool for corporate communicators.

The impact of a story told through video depends on three things:

✓ The emotive power of the story being told

✓ The quality of the way it's told

✓ The power of the medium through which it's told (in this case, video)

As corporate communicators, we're always looking to create projects that will be remembered and acted on by our target audience. The way that information is shared makes a significant difference to its overall impact. Because of this, it's important to understand what makes a great story.

Simply put, a story is the encapsulation of cause and effect: A leads to B, B leads to C, etc. Good stories include a degree of conflict. Instead of A obviously leading to B, it may lead to E, F or even G. The greater the amount at stake, or the degree of jeopardy, the more engaging the narrative.

Good stories engage the audience because the audience empathise with the subjects. The best stories reflect primal narratives that exist within our psyches. Most ancient myths feature a hero figure triumphing against overwhelming odds. This is a story that all humans feel is relevant to them.

Stories are useful for businesses looking to develop a brand, because they provide a central narrative that members of the audience can decide to align with. Native Americans have used a shared narrative to align different members of their hunting parties around a shared goal.

This matters to you because modern brands use stories in the same way. Video is the best way of telling a compelling story online. The reason for this is that video is a fundamentally emotive medium. It works best as a tool to generate an emotional response in the audience.

One of the main reasons for this is that our brains subconsciously feel the same emotions we're witnessing on screen. It has been shown that the audience of intense psychological thrillers featuring subjects suffering the effects of schizophrenia temporarily exhibit the same brain chemistry as someone experiencing a psychotic episode. This feature makes video an extremely effective tool for marketers, hence the continuing success of TV advertising.

In order to achieve this effect, though, it must be produced well enough for the audience to be able to overlook the knowledge that they are consuming a construct. They must be able to suspend their disbelief.

CHAPTER 2

THE DEMOCRATISATION OF VIDEO

At the turn of this century, if you wanted to share information with a geographically diverse group, you had limited options, and these generally cost money – quite a lot of it. This made mass communication a luxury that was only really available to those with deep pockets. The Internet has obviously changed that. Each website has a potentially global reach – the odd totalitarian firewall notwithstanding. Social media platforms are all designed to make the broadcasting of information as simple as possible for their participants. Through smartphones, the sharing and consuming of that information can happen anywhere.

It's important that you understand how this will affect your business and brand, because it's possible that you're wasting an opportunity to build more-effective connections with your stakeholders. At the very least, you may not be investing your budget in the best way possible. I've worked with many businesses that have been able to get significantly better returns with just a few small tweaks.

To help you to understand what they might be, this chapter looks at the following:

>>   A revolution in means requires a revolution in strategy

>>   Who's doing this really well?

>>   Brands as broadcasters

A Revolution in Means Requires a Revolution in Strategy

Filming and editing equipment used to cost a fortune. A camera and lenses could easily be US$200,000, and an editing station was pretty much the same price. The money alone was a significant barrier to entry to anyone wanting to make their own professional-grade film. If you could afford to buy the kit and learn how to use it, you could call yourself a production company and you'd have a pretty decent paying job for life. That was until around 2004–2007, when a tidal wave of technology swept through moving-image production, pulling fees and costs down through the floor.

Cameras everywhere

Initially, there were camcorders, then DSLRs (stills cameras shooting video), and now there are HD camera phones, drones and 360° cameras, which can be bought with a few months' wages from a paper round (if they still exist?). Who knows what new kit visual storytellers will be using in 10 years' time? There is an old photography adage that, "The best camera is the one that you have on you". Now the majority of the global population have the best camera they could ever want, because they carry camera phones everywhere they go. They can shoot, edit and upload video from almost anywhere in the world, and they're doing it with a device that is regular consumer technology. This completely changes the game in terms of the ubiquity, quality and accessibility of filmmaking. It means that, in a very short period of time, brands have had to completely change their approach to the format.

Semaphore to 4G

The beeping, whirring world of the early, dial-up Internet may as well have been semaphore as far as video was concerned. It wasn't until around 2005 that the Internet became fast enough to host video functionally (even if the early videos were the size of postage stamps). YouTube was founded in the December of that year. Now we can stream 4K video to our mobile phones, almost anywhere, over the 4G network. In the 10 years from 2007–2016, the average amount of time each person spent online nearly quadrupled from just over 1 hour a day to over 3.5.[1;2]

That blistering revolution has happened in just over a decade, and it has drastically changed the way you need to think about video as a business tool. Combined with the democratisation of production, this puts the power of video, as covered in the last chapter, into the hands of the majority of humanity. Many people have seized on this capability and used it to their advantage, as we will see. The problem for too many businesses is that they have marketing strategies that are simple evolutions of those that worked when the communications world was unidirectional. A revolution in means requires a revolution in strategy.

Where does video sit vs other channels?

"I suppose it is tempting, if the only tool you have is a hammer, to treat everything as if it were a nail."

– Abraham Maslow, the law of the instrument

I'm focusing on video in this book because I know it, I understand it and I respect its capabilities. I don't want to fall into the trap of suggesting that it is right in every instance or that it doesn't benefit from being supported with cross promotion from other platforms. What I am sure of, though, is that no modern marketing or branding strategy can be complete without video as a central plank. Because of this, a well-thought-out, effective, video-led strategy is essential to maximising your brand's impact in the modern world.

On top of the traditional, offline channels, which have been enhanced by increased technology, online advances have created a mind-bending array of different ways to connect with your audience. Different social platforms, websites and apps vie with the importance of face-to-face contact at offline events, direct marketing and a resurgent desire for the tangibility of print.

All of these are relevant to the modern business communicator. The key is that you get them to all 'sing from the same hymn sheet'; i.e. they should be used in concert with brand messages and an identity that is consistent across all of them. You should try to think of each of these as complementing one another. If this is done effectively, then they offer you the opportunity to drive engagement to ever-higher levels.

Using the Channel – Raqqa is Being Slaughtered Silently (RIBSS)

The ubiquitous nature of the camera and distribution platform has empowered a wide range of different groups that didn't have a mouthpiece before. This is having a significant impact on news and current affairs. An excellent example of this is by the group known as Raqqa is Being Slaughtered Silently (RIBSS or RBSS), which was set up following the invasion of the Northern Syrian city of Raqqa by Islamic State of Iraq and Syria (ISIS) in 2012. A group of local citizen journalists saw that the story of what was happening there was being passed over by the international news agenda. They realised that this was due to the fact that getting news material out of the city was almost impossible. At the time, ISIS was broadcasting the story that it had been welcomed into the city as a liberator by the local population. This could not have been further from the truth. RIBSS set about doing what it could to correct the narrative.

The group set up a website and a Facebook page for sharing their stories of living in ISIS's caliphate. At terminal risk to their own safety, the group members videoed, photographed and wrote about the different aspects of living under the occupation, from public executions to queues to get drinking water. Through doing this, they were able to use their channel to raise awareness of the reality of the situation. A number of the group members have been tortured and murdered, but they are internationally recognised as providing uniquely valuable insights into life in Raqqa – they stopped the world forgetting about what was happening in their home. A small group of people with some cameras and an Internet connection had the ability to defy one of the most oppressive and perverted regimes to exist. This would not have been possible 10 years earlier.

If people can create a cohesive presence using material that they produced at mortal risk to their own safety, you can do this with everything that you have to hand. You just need to want to do it.

The quality content bar has been raised

These revolutions are already having knock-on effects – for example, the bar for what constitutes high quality has shifted upwards significantly. From Netflix to HBO, and Amazon Prime to network on demand, broadband Internet has substantially increased the amount of excellent content available. From live sports coverage to stunning wildlife documentaries, new technology is enabling a level of access and production values that were pretty much unimaginable just a few years ago. We're living through the golden age of glossy TV.

These technological advancements aren't limited to improvements in two-dimensional (2D) video. There is now 360° video/virtual reality (VR), augmented reality (AR), and interactive video. Each of these technologies could have a chapter to itself. While they are still at a relatively primitive stage compared to where they will be, they represent new and ever-improving ways of providing immersive stories to the audience. They are a goldmine for corporate communicators who are willing to push them and use them with a little creative flair. They provide an opportunity for a different type of immersion in your brand narrative from what was possible before – enhancing and enriching the stories that you choose to tell around your brand. As we previously covered, having an effective brand narrative is essential to modern businesses. These new technologies provide additional platforms for you to bring this narrative to life.

On a practical level, the ubiquity of quality content and hands-on filmmaking opportunities have made your audience, both internal and external, far more filmically literate than they were. On the one hand, they are more willing to look past shortcomings in quality when seeking out the value they're looking for in the video, but, on the other hand, their perception of what constitutes 'good' filmmaking has risen significantly. This means that the video work you produce needs to perform at a higher level – it has to be really good. That isn't to say that it necessarily needs to be glossy and/or expensive, but it does need to be well conceived and well executed: strategically and creatively. Most of all, though, it must provide value to the audience. We'll cover that in more depth shortly.

What Can You Learn From Video Bloggers: YouTubers

As previously discussed, social media has given a communication channel to all of us who choose to use it. Whether we're sharing photos, likes, tweets, updates, comments or videos, it's all broadcasting. Some people have got really good at this – they are uploading the kind of compelling content that people want to see, and doing so consistently enough to build a following. Some of them have regular audiences that run into the tens of millions – figures that most traditional broadcast channels would kill for. These video bloggers or 'YouTubers' have arisen as a new form of celebrity.

They are interesting to us because they are the archetype of the citizen broadcaster. They are at the forefront of the video revolution. Because of this, there are a few important things that we can learn from their success:

- ✓ **The importance of understanding your audience**
- ✓ **You can achieve great things even with limited resources**
- ✓ **The power of the niche in the online world**
- ✓ **Consistency is key**

The importance of understanding your audience

If the success of online video bloggers shows us anything, it's the power of understanding your audience. They are members of the audience demographic, who have been able to take up the tools and create content that perfectly resonates with their peers. They know exactly what will make their audience tick, what angle to take and what is important/irrelevant. Their tone of voice and language are perfectly suited to those they're broadcasting to.

Whatever you're looking to achieve with your communications, you need to close the understanding gap between you and your audience. The more airtight the understanding, the greater the chance that what you're saying will engage and ring true with your audience. There are lots of different ways of gaining this understanding – focus groups, consulting with or including members of the target audience in the ideation/production, and even employing them can help you get the tone and content just right. Whatever you do, though, don't try to fake it.

A quick note on this...

In many cases, what will work for the audience may not be what works for the executives who ultimately sign off on the campaign. Many potentially excellent projects become compromised because stakeholders who aren't part of the target demographic don't like things such as the music, the font or the dialogue. *If you're not the target audience, it's not meant for you, so don't mess with it.* Making changes like this damage the authenticity of the project in the audience's eyes and limit its effectiveness.

Achieving great things with limited resources

It goes without saying that bedroom video bloggers are working with limited resources. The point here is that you don't need a vast budget to do the things that you need to do. Limitations in budget, time and logistics can be worked around, because filmmaking is a flexible, creative process. The whole point of the democratisation of quality video is that what you have can go so much further.

That isn't to say that you should be cheap in your approach, just that you should be definite in what you're trying to achieve and be creative in how you achieve it. If all you're looking for is literally a video for your homepage, then of course you should just shoot, edit and upload it yourself. You will have achieved your aim. If you're looking to achieve something specific as a result of having it there – an increase in click-throughs or requests for information, for example – then you might want to look at working with a professional. You'll get a tangibly better product that will give a better account of your business. The quality of the creative messaging accounts for up to 75% of the effectiveness of the output.[3;4] There is naturally an opportunity cost to any work that you share, so make sure it's as good as it can be. There is more on the economics of video production in Chapter 5. To summarise now, though, you wouldn't let an intern paint your office, so don't let them make you look amateurish online.

The power of the niche in the online world

One of the marvels of the online world is that the potential audience is so vast that there is always the scope to find a followership, no matter how niche your focus might be. In fact, the more specialist and tailored you can be, the more likely you are to find and engage an audience; just make sure the content is relevant and interesting for the audience. We examine the niche further in Chapter 7.

Consistency is key

None of the video bloggers (who weren't already well known/famous) achieved their success overnight. They started by making movies from their bedrooms, and just kept going – day after day, week after week, year after year. They put many hours into producing, shooting and editing their videos every day, even initially when there was just a handful of people watching them. Over time, they kept going, sharing material that was consistent and of value to their audience, and that audience grew. From the humblest of acorns grow the mightiest of oaks.

This is important for business communicators because our mentality is usually focused on far-shorter timeframes. But, for the most part, to build a real following for your online channel you need to work consistently for a period of months.

To build the kind of brand loyalty that is achievable requires months, if not years, of following, tweaking and evolving your content plan, as required.

How you make these points work for you is covered in the next two chapters.

Paying for influence

DO YOUR HOMEWORK AND BE SELECTIVE ABOUT THE INFLUENCERS YOU WORK WITH

The high numbers of subscribers to video bloggers' channels and the fact that their audience has a very specific demographic profile makes them very attractive as influencer marketers. Across the online space, people who have built followings are able to leverage these with endorsements of products and services, which brands are willing to pay handsomely for. A video blog by someone respected among your target audience will potentially keep returning value to you for years to come. It can be challenging to build an audience, so what could be easier than simply buying into someone else's?

There are a few things to help you get the most from this approach:

1. **Authenticity is key in influencer marketing.** If the audience gets the impression that the influencer is not being honest with the information that they share, it damages the influencer and your brand. Because of this, be prepared for them to be honest in the way that they talk about your product. Of course, talk to them

about what they plan to include, but if you're not happy with it, be prepared to walk away rather than make them damage the whole enterprise with dishonesty.

2. **Be targeted.** Do your homework on the influencers that your audience are engaged with. Make sure that they have a strong connection to your subject matter. There are thousands of influencers out there, so you can afford to be selective.

3. **Don't necessarily go for the biggest name you can afford.** While it might be tempting to blow a significant budget on a big name or sector celebrity, you might find it more useful to go with a number of people with smaller followings, but whom you may be able to get more time or focus from. A few hundred thousand on a tweet from Kim Kardashian might put you in front of a big audience, but it's probably more useful to get someone who'll devote time and thought to working with you.

4. **Influencers are individuals.** They are looking for ways to build their own brand and celebrity. Look for ways in which you can use your network to achieve what they are after, and you'll get far more from them. Taking a moment to understand the value transfer that is going on is time well spent.

5. **Be clear on exactly what is expected.** Be prepared to explain this face-to-face/in a one pager rather than having it buried in a contract that might not be read. I've worked on a campaign where, halfway through, one of the young influencers took to their Instagram account to bemoan corporate influence and selling out. Not what the brand that had paid top dollar had quite bargained for. Make sure that everyone is clear on the deliverables and rules at the outset, and it'll pay back.

There are challenges around influencer marketing, though:

»   **Transparency with the audience.** There has been some criticism of influencers for not always being completely transparent about whether or not they are being paid to feature and promote products.

This has led to a campaign to include in the video #Ad or a strapline explaining that the content has been funded by a third party.

» **Tracking return on investment can be difficult.** Yes, you know that a certain number of people have engaged with the content, but how do you know if/how these converted to doing what you wanted them to?

» **Mark-ups from vendors.** There has been an explosion in influencer-marketing companies. All of these make significant promises of audience growth and engagement. It can be difficult to know exactly what you're paying for, though. Mark-ups in the sector are notoriously high, so make sure you aren't being stung.

» **Limitations with the format.** There are limits to the amount a brand can achieve by piggybacking on the success and notoriety of others. There may well be a very strong value and purpose match with the endorser (i.e. they may fit perfectly into the brand's story), in which case influencers can be effective. But, as a general rule, paying people to feature you on their own channel should only be used to build your own audience, and complement the brand story you are telling effectively elsewhere and on other channels.

The best thing to do if you're hoping to make influencer marketing part of your offering is to speak to an expert. There are a number of companies out there that specialise in this, or you can drop me an email and I'd be very happy to point you in the right direction/help.

Becoming a Brand Broadcaster

Many brands have taken advantage of these evolutions to take on the role of broadcasters in their own right. They are using the capability to share stories, build positive brand associations and use video to help them accomplish their business strategies. These businesses don't think in discrete, cyclical campaigns, but in a rolling, evolving journey for their audience – much like a traditional network TV channel. There are – of course – quick wins to be had, and video can drive very immediate results, which is all that the majority of businesses are going to use it for, and that's fine. There is no reason why your business can't transform its standing in the market on the back of a carefully considered, creative video strategy. To do that, you need to start thinking a little longer term.

Shift your mindset: Marketing as a product

> *"There are only two things in a business that make money –*
> *innovation and marketing. Everything else is a cost."*
>
> – Peter Drucker, 'the creator of modern management'[5]

The most important shift towards thinking like a broadcaster is to appreciate and value your content as an additional product that your organisation creates. Broadcasters, of course, have to think like that as it's their only output. Whatever your company produces, if you're serious about building your brand's cachet, you need to think of your content as another element of your product offering to your customers. In your audience's minds, it's difficult to unpick the different elements that make up your brand. If you create and share material that hasn't been properly thought through or is poor quality, what does that say about the rest of the things that your business produces? There was a time in the early days of having video online when you could be forgiven for producing substandard work. That time has passed – you'll find that even some of the youngest members of your audience can produce decent-looking video. Because of this, it's important that your content looks and sounds the part.

Just as poor-quality video can damage your brand, so can high-quality video increase the value of your brand. This potential to build brand value is such that you're leaving money on the table by not considering the content you share to be of equal importance to your other products.

Shift your mindset: Timeframes

The other shift is towards a more consistent, longer-term distribution cadence. Traditional marketing tends to take place on a 12–18-month moving cycle. There is a summer campaign and a Christmas/holiday-season campaign, and between the two there has tended to be a bit of a break while everyone takes stock and ramps up for the next one. This is largely the effect of the quarterly and annual reporting cycle that all businesses adhere to. It may well take a longer period to build the depth of brand affinity with your audience that being a broadcaster has the potential to give you access to.

Traditional broadcasters tend to think in decades. They aim to engage viewers in their mid-to-late teens, and then keep them, with different types of programming, throughout their lives. Now, of course, this is completely unrealistic as a timeframe for the majority of businesses, but the evolution of content that a network offers over a lifetime can be condensed into the different types of content that you should share over a prospective customer's sales-lifecycle journey.

Long-term business value relies on finding, keeping and growing customers who come back to our brands for years. We want to build affinities with our products that are passed down, generation to generation. We do that by becoming so much more to our consumers than just a soap or shoe supplier. We want our products to be as useful to our customers as they possibly can be, so why not aim to make the content that supports them as helpful as possible too? We want to provide the customer with as much value as we economically can – whether that is in the quality of your physical product, or in the material that you share to support and promote it.

Generating value: Perceived vs real – Ludwig von Mises

Before you start questioning the point of adding value to your product with video, consider that, in the mind of the audience, there is no difference between 'real' and 'perceived' value; i.e. the value that is in the quality of the product and the value that is added through marketing, respectively. So, it's generally a lot easier and cheaper to add value to the product by making it desirable to your audience through positive branding than it is to make your product proportionally better.

Ludwig von Mises

This is reflected in the work of Austrian-American social economist Ludwig von Mises. He argues that it's impossible to split the enjoyment of a diner between the quality of the food cooked by the chef in a restaurant and the value provided by the man who sweeps the restaurant's floors.[6] Ogilvy vice chairman, Rory Sutherland, rather sharpens the understanding of this by saying that it would be impossible to enjoy a meal if there were a strong smell of effluent coming from the loos; i.e. it wouldn't matter how great the chef, the ingredients or the food were, if you couldn't shake the smell of sewage.

This has been the role of marketing since the beginning. The point of this chapter has been to show you that it's now easier than ever to add perceived value to your brand and product(s) with video. The next two chapters will show you how you can do this.

What you Can Learn from A Brand Broadcaster: Red Bull

Some of the more advanced businesses in this area are starting to build brand presences that have transcended the association with their original product. Energy-drinks manufacturer Red Bull is probably the most obvious of these. With its *Red Bull Media House*, it creates thousands of pieces of content, has correspondents in 160 countries, distributes one of the most popular magazines in the world and has its own TV channel. I'm not suggesting that this is quite how far you should go. It's more that it's a useful guide as to just how much like a traditional broadcaster a brand can end up being.

Nearly all the content that the Red Bull Media House produces is only obliquely relevant to the original brand. The link is with the initial core aim of the brand, in that Red Bull gives wings to people and their ideas – 'Red Bull gives you wings'. I'll come on to how you can think about the different types of content you might want to produce in the next chapter. But there are three things that you can take from Red Bull's approach to content production:

✓ **Take the leap**

✓ **Prepare for the long term**

✓ **It needs to come from the top**

Take the leap

Like a motocross rider about to pull a backflip on Red Bull's channel, if you're going to do it, you need to commit. Their failure to do this might mean they land on their head; you may just end up wasting your time and money. For many companies, though, this will require a real step away from what they are used to. Red Bull really went for it and has built an entirely new multi-billion-dollar category as a result. This culminated in Red Bull Media House's crowning achievement, which is arguably Felix Baumgartner's jump from the edge of space, which was watched by a live global audience of nearly 8 million. The photo of him having landed safely on the Red Bull Facebook page was liked by 466,000 people. That is a lot of engagement! All of the additional material that the jump generated enabled members of the audience to take, repurpose and own elements of the story, in the digitoral tradition as previously discussed.

Prepare for the long term

Red Bull first launched its content wing in 2007 – it has taken it 10 years to achieve the dominance in the space that it has now. Over that time, it has taken a sustained approach to building its audience and the loyalty of its many followers; this has led to a significant and measurable increase in the value of the Red Bull brand. The problem with trying to account for this using a traditional marketing framework is that it's almost impossible to calculate the increase in brand value on a piece-by-piece basis. While any brand can benefit from having a more joined-up content strategy, being a brand broadcaster is a long-term investment in your company's future value.

It needs to come from the top

> Everyone wants to be Apple,
> but no one wants to be Steve Jobs

The reason I wrote this book is that I've had so many conversations with people in companies like yours, where they say they agree with much of what I have to say, but they really struggle to get sign-off from the executive team.

One of the main challenges for businesses wanting to capitalise on the opportunity that is on offer to them is misunderstanding or fear among the executive team. There is no reason why any company that chooses to can't achieve excellent returns, but it has to come from the top. Red Bull has two shareholders – the original entrepreneurs who set the business up. That means it has the freedom to make the decisions that are in the long-term interest of the brand. It can choose to take the calculated risks that are necessary to make this stuff really work, without having to answer to the drive for short-term returns. So many of the companies that I've spoken to want to be Apple – they love the Apple brand, the precision of its operations and the adoration of its users (and its profit margin!) – but no one is prepared to be Steve Jobs: risk taking, brave and uncompromising in his pursuit for perfection. To expect one without the other is unrealistic and naïve.

In Summary: The Democratisation of Video

In this chapter, we've looked at how advances in both camera and online-distribution technology have given us all our own content channel to use as we see fit. The people who have done really well out of these advances are video bloggers. They are (predominantly) young people who have built an online following by consistently sharing videos that provide value for their audience.

Video bloggers are important to us because they illustrate four key concepts:

1. **You don't need vast resources to build an effective following online.** Many of the most successful bloggers are still in their teens/early twenties. Don't be cheap, though; quality is important.

2. **The vast audience that the online environment offers allows broadcasters to be extremely niche in the content they share.** This actually strengthens their standing with the right audience. Anything you can create content about can be shared and used to build an audience.

3. **As actual members of their audience demographic, they have an innate sense of what will and won't work for the audience.** This is what they will find interesting, useful and amusing. You need to get as close to a perfect understanding of your target audience as possible, in order to create content that will be as effective as it can possibly be.

4. **Being consistent is essential to building a loyal following.** The audience want to know what they're going to get and when they're going to get it. To build long-term business value requires a long-term plan that is then delivered on.

Finally, brands have not missed out on these advances. We're only just starting to see the potential that the future holds for brands that want to build an engaged audience with their communications. There are some important shifts that need to happen for interested businesses to be able to maximise on this. The most important of these, by some margin, is a shift in thinking to a longer-term, more sustained approach to building their brand in the eyes of the audience.

You need to start to think beyond this quarter's or next quarter's results, and focus on a three-, five- or ten-year timeframe, much like a traditional broadcaster.

In the next chapter, we're going to look at what you should *actually* be broadcasting on your channels.

CHAPTER 3

WHAT YOU SHOULD BE BROADCASTING

Over the last two chapters, we've covered what makes video a particularly effective tool for business storytellers. We've looked at some of the ways that it's been used to drive action – the key aim for any corporate communicator and at how advances in technology have put this powerful capability in the hands of individuals and businesses alike.

Hopefully, you now understand the opportunity that video content gives you to increase the value of your brand; value that your customers will ultimately pay you for. In this chapter, I'd like to spend a little time looking at what you should be broadcasting. The first thing to define in any strategy is what result you're trying to achieve. Once you've made this clear, you can start to think about how you achieve it.

Thinking About Your Audience

> Your target audience can be defined as the people you need to influence to fulfil your business objective.

These may be the people who will take the action you require (e.g. applying to your apprenticeship programme) or those who will influence the people who will take the action (friends, family, colleagues, teachers, etc.). As with the overall objectives for your content, these should be defined by your business objectives.

Tailoring what you share to your target audience is essential, no matter what communication medium you're using. This is fundamental to maximising the impact of your spend. I've included a methodology for defining your output and tailoring to your audience in Chapter 7. For now, just remember that it's important for you to understand your target audience as well as you possibly can when considering the material you'll share. As we saw when looking at the success of video bloggers your success will be defined by your ability to create content that resonates with them. This requires research and leg work to get it just right, but it's the starting point for any successful campaign.

Don't Assume Knowledge

During my brief period working at BBC News, they ran a series of focus groups looking at all the news content that the corporation shared. This ranged from their highbrow, flagship shows such as the *Today* radio programme and heavy-hitting *Newsnight*, through the more-daytime-TV *Breakfast* and *Six O'clock News*, and on to *Newsround* – the children's news show that plays at the end of children's TV at 5.30pm. The members of the group were a cross section of society, being of all ages, socioeconomic backgrounds and geographic areas. The most popular programme – by some margin – was *Newsround*: the kids' show!

This was because it was easy to understand and, crucially, didn't rely on any background knowledge. Every story was explained in simple steps, which made them accessible for the majority of the audience that dip into stories. The problem for the BBC (and all news organisations) is that the news is produced by people who eat, sleep and breathe what is going on in the world. They tend to make programmes for themselves, just as far too many marketers make marketing campaigns for themselves. Don't assume that your audience know anything about your product. They know a lot less than you think. Make it really easy for them to understand what you're sharing with them, and they will thank you for it.

Internal/external audiences

Another change that has taken place as a result of the ubiquity of video, which we looked at in the last chapter, is that there is no longer a significant dividing line between the internal and external audiences of your brand. The field of employer branding has been a significant growth area over the last 10 years or so. The idea is that if your people are the personification of your brand to your customer base, it's important that they are all clued up as to what the business stands for. Platforms like the website Glassdoor (which lets employees share what they think of you as an employer) have dissolved the internal/external brand distinction even further.

The reason I mention this is that you need to make sure you think of your internal audience as a discerning audience in their own right. In the 1970s and 1980s, head office could get away with sending out a VHS tape, and their various company departments would sit in smoke-filled, magnolia-painted rooms and watch it. In the unidirectional-communications environment, they had no choice. In the modern world, though, the content you produce for your internal communications is judged by the same yardstick as anything else your audience watches. It still has to pass the 'what's in it for me/is this a load of rubbish' test, before the audience will engage with it. I want to underline that this isn't about spending lots of money. It concerns thinking carefully about what you're trying to get across, and having a clear strategy to achieve this. Don't underestimate the savvy and discernment of your staff; it will lead to less-effective work and a wasted investment – of their time and your money.

Content Marketing

The Internet has sped up our lives – email has turned airmail into 'snail mail'. Mobile Internet connectivity has made our lives faster still. We're being robbed of the last shreds of time we had to think. The pace of life, and the profusion of different channels and distractions has sharpened our perception of the value of our time. As marketers, this poses a challenge for getting our communications heard. Along with this heightened awareness, the audience has control of how they invest their time, and, with the prevalence of ad-blocking software (see the next box), marketing messages face a challenge to be noticed. For us to achieve cut-through (landing our message with the audience), our content has to pass over a higher 'is this a valuable use of my time' bar than ever. This has led to a dramatic resurgence of marketing content that has its own inherent value; i.e. content marketing.

> *"Content marketing is a technique of creating and distributing valuable, relevant and consistent content to attract and acquire a clearly defined audience – with the objective of driving profitable customer action."*
>
> – The Content Marketing Institute

Content now has to deliver value to the audience in its own right. Content marketing, by contrast, builds affinity between the audience and the brand through providing this value. As opposed to 'sales activation' content – 'buy this product now!' – which aims to sell the product or service directly.

> Content marketing works online because it provides a clear answer to the audience's 'What's in it for me?' (WIIFM) question.

This has led to an explosion in content marketing, from a quality that rivals (and in some places exceeds) the producing company's original product to the 'click-bait' nonsense that makes up the majority of spammy blogs, videos and posts.

> *"89% of B2B marketers and 86% of B2C marketers are using content marketing... 75% of marketers are increasing investment in content marketing"*
>
> – Impact Brand, 2017[1]

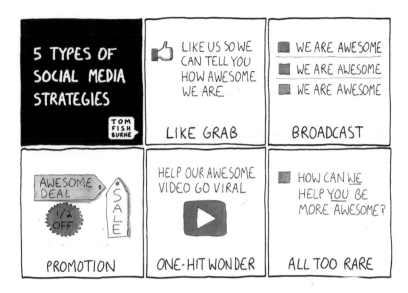

LIKE MANY OF TOM FISHBURNE'S EXCELLENT CARTOONS, THIS ONE NAILS AN IMPORTANT TRUTH THAT ALL MARKETERS SHOULD TAKE GUIDANCE FROM

Ad Blockers

Ad-blocking software is designed to detect advertisements and stop them appearing on the user's screen. This means that the user doesn't have the distraction of advertising messaging popping up and spoiling their online experience. The software is extremely damaging for the online publishing industry, which relies on advertising for its revenue and, ultimately, its existence. Around 11% of the global Internet population are blocking ads on the web.[2] This will cost publishers an estimated US$27 billion annually by 2020.[3] Marketers should bear some of the responsibility for this, as they have grown up partially as a result of the poor-quality, annoying marketing that users have sought respite from.

> This has led to marketers looking for ways to incorporate their brands into the content the user is accessing, in the form of product placements or onscreen endorsements. The prevalence of this type of programme makes content with its own intrinsic value an even more essential tool in the armoury of the marketer of the future.
>
> *"More than 615 million devices now have ad-blocking software."*
> – PageFair, 2017 Global Adblock Report[4]

A simple way of thinking about providing value for your audience

Content marketing is about delivering 'value' to the audience. What do we actually mean by that? Marketing guru Seth Godin describes it as follows:

> *"...something that people would seek out, and that they would miss if it wasn't there."*[5]

In terms of thinking about your content, a simple guide to this is that the audience are looking for something that is TRUE; that is, timely, relevant, useful or entertaining. The better you understand your audience, the more effective the content that you create for them will be. We'll come on to that in more depth in Chapter 7. Let's look at what is meant by each of those terms:

Timely

Timing is key to effective content. Think about how successful Oreo was with its 'You Can Dunk in the Dark' tweet, when the lights went out during the 2013 Super Bowl. It was picked up by the 23 million Twitter users who were watching the game, and ended up being regarded as the ad of the evening – a title that many companies had spent millions of dollars for a shot at, and failed. It goes without saying that what is timely for one viewer is annoyingly late for another – the correct advice 30 seconds after you've made a decision is annoying.

Relevant

As we touched on previously, the content has to be relevant to the audience. This almost goes without saying – we all constantly filter the information that assails us every waking moment. Because of this, your audience are keenly aware of what does and doesn't apply to them. Think about what is going to be relevant for your viewers – this might now be directly obvious. For example, if you're trying to market an apprentice scheme to school leavers, they may be interested in advice on renting a home for the first time. This information is obviously not so interesting to those looking to move job as an experienced hire. This underlines the importance of understanding your audience and what is relevant to them.

A word of warning here, according to research by LinkedIn, 44% of their respondents said they would consider ending a relationship with a brand because of irrelevant promotions. An additional 22% said that they would 'definitely defect' from that brand.[6] Knowing your audience and making content that is relevant to them is essential.

Useful

One step on from being relevant is content that is actually useful. Providing how-tos, instructions, discounts and tie-ins with other products that they may be using are all ways of being useful to your audience. Once again, what is useful to your viewers might not be immediately obvious – look at the previous example. Home-renting advice is also useful to the target audience. These different types of value don't exist in isolation – each piece of content can be a combination of one or more things.

Entertaining

We all need a little entertainment from time to time. If you can get it right, this is a great way of drawing in your audience and winning them over. Tread carefully with this though – you have to make sure that whatever you share ties in with your brand. You need to earn the trust of the audience before making drastic departures in tone of voice. There is more on tone and style a little later in this chapter.

The content you produce doesn't need to be all of those things at the same time – any one or two will work, as long as it/they provide enough value in that given area. The more entertaining and relevant your work content is, for example, the more the chance there is that it will be watched, shared and loved.

Different ways of skinning a cat

Google defines the different ways of engaging your audience with your content slightly differently[7]:

» **Inspire** the audience with *emotional* and *relatable* stories

» **Educate** the audience with *useful information*

» **Entertain** the audience by *surprising them, making them laugh* or *sharing spectacular content*

There's no right or wrong way of looking at these; they are just a different way of looking at the same underlying principles. I hope that seeing them from a slightly different angle will help you to understand them and use them.

Quality vs quantity

As an established brand, online visitors will expect you to have a decent, video-led web presence. Don't fall into the trap of just creating and sharing any old material because the space is there. There was a stage where the prevailing wisdom seemed to be that these platforms were effectively a content void, that needed to be filled with whatever might be available. This has led to some significant household-name businesses sharing very-poor-quality material online – which is badly filmed, badly thought out, too long, too banal and too badly organised. This colours what visitors think of your business, harming your standing.

To minimise this risk, you should focus on quality over quantity. Not necessarily high production quality, but at least high concept quality. Technological advancement has put quality production in the hands of your staff – just make sure they put time and thought into using it. Efficiently curated videos, ideally on your own website or hosted on YouTube, can take a big step towards fulfilling the potential that video holds for your brand.

Defining your channel brand or tone

All content has a style or tone. Think about how the different traditional broadcasters have their own tone or brand. Just as the tone of Fox News differs from the BBC, so should you establish your own channel's tone. To begin with, I'd recommend that your content's tone conforms to your broader brand. Over time, you may find that it can start to diverge. This is understandable – and may be desirable – but it should be a function of you gaining the trust of the audience and then pushing it incrementally. First and foremost, the content you share must feel authentic to the audience.

Once you've decided what the brand is going to be, it's worth setting down some brand guidelines to keep you on track over time. This can vary from the technical (e.g. what resolutions you should film in) and the aesthetic (e.g. colour schemes) to the tone of voice (e.g. how you should talk).

Once you have a guide of all the things the channel should do or say, it's worth making a list of all the things that it shouldn't. Now test it. Does what you're saying sound right? Does it sound authentically like your brand? You might want to share your thoughts with a few people, particularly some members of the target audience.

Remember that the brand is a living thing, so it may well evolve over time. Keep in mind that whatever you share has to feel authentic to the audience. Nothing will end in painful shame faster than your brand doing the marketing equivalent of 'dad dancing'. If you can find a message that really resonates with your audience, they can and will amplify it many times over. You should look for content that presents this opportunity. Unfortunately, if you get it wrong, it can work against you in exactly the opposite way.

Using Your Business Values and Purpose to Inform Your Content

It can be a little baffling to think about all the different types of content you might want to make. A useful way to start (and I'll go into a lot more detail on this in the next chapter) is by looking at your business's values and purpose. All the content that you create (no matter how disparate the actual subject matter) should be in some way a physical manifestation of your purpose and brand values. For example, Red Bull's purpose is to give wings to people and their ideas. This is manifested in the nature of the types of people, sports and events that it features on its channel.

If you can follow this rule, your content will be far more cohesive in its nature and will do a more effective job of building your brand equity. Whatever your corporate purpose, your channel gives you an unrivalled opportunity to make something that is, by its nature, intangible into something tangible.

> *"Be yourself. Everyone else is already taken."*
>
> – Oscar Wilde

Keeping It Real: Allianz #CarStories – Case Study

We look at the role of authenticity in the next chapter. However, it's worth looking at a brief case study now. Allianz insurance wanted to promote the fact that, by providing car insurance, it facilitates all the family time that gets spent in cars. It was an interesting insight on what could be seen as a fairly dry, but essential, product. Initially, it asked its advertising agency to create a commercial to promote this message. It set to work, spending an eye-watering budget on expensive crews, actors, locations, lighting and equipment.

Where it really went wrong was in using actors to play the family. Despite the fact that they did a decent job, the viewer can immediately identify that the film feels contrived and bogus. It doesn't chime with our own gut sense of how a family interacts. Allianz ended up pulling the commercial after a week.

As part of the online activation, Casual worked with Allianz's below-the-line agency to create something a little more heartfelt. The films focus on a series of real families driving in their cars and talking about different subjects, from the safari park to when the parents brought the new baby home for the first time. The families were interviewed in depth by a producer beforehand, to judge their appropriateness and the potential subjects they could feature.

Having chosen the right families, the team then removed as much of the production crew and equipment from the cars as was feasible. The goal here was to allow the families to be as normal and genuine in their interactions as possible. To do this, they used a 'fixed rig' of cameras in the car to record the family from a number of angles. The production team travelled in the car behind, recording sound and feeding the family discussion topics.

The resulting 14 45-second videos were featured on the company's Facebook page, where the heartfelt interactions and kids' funny statements made them a massive hit. Their short length and poignant content made them particularly touching. On YouTube, the videos got an 87% view-completion rate – which is practically unheard of – this is so high that Google got in touch with us to ask us how we had managed it.

The only answer was that, having chosen the 'right' families, we removed as much of the artifice as possible and let the family interactions speak for themselves. It's amazing what you can get when you set the cameras up and have the confidence to just let real life happen.

What Can Video be Used For?

One of the major challenges we had when we started Casual was that video can be used for such a wide range of things. Before we realised the importance of focus, we'd answer the question "So, what can you make films about?" with the pretty useless "Almost anything". Over time, we learned to be a bit more specific, and, in the last 10 years, we've made films that bring the whole of the employee lifestyle to life, from initial awareness, through recruitment, and on to ongoing engagement, and learning and development. We've even made films that retain and build a network of alumni for those who've moved on. We've made product promotions, adverts, discount films, branded content and conference openers. Some of these with actors and others with online influencers, with helicopters, drones and bodycams.

Casual has made over 8,000 different films for almost everything a company could want a film for. It's really important to understand that film or moving image can enhance any message you might have to share. As we learned in Chapter 1, video is a great way of weaving emotion into selected facts. This increases their impact, memorability and the chance that people will act on them. Let's look at some of the ways that video has been used by corporate communicators. We use the following classifications at Casual to separate all the different things that our clients have used our work for in the past. This isn't exhaustive, but it does give a picture of the breadth of uses. Some of these are quite similar – or even overlap – and rely on similar attributes of video for their effectiveness.

Boost sales

> *"Shoppers who view video are 1.81x more likely to purchase than non-viewers."*
>
> – Adobe, 2015[8]

The most common films made by companies, which we see in our day-to-day lives, are those designed to sell things. From the dawn of TV, advertisers have been promoting their wares, using every trick in the filmmaker's book to introduce, promote and explain their products. Films that are able to do this remain the kings of corporate films. From the time in the 1940s and 1950s when advertisers were able to show that there is a direct line of correlation between the amount spent and sales increases, the budgets for these short films have grown, in some cases to become eye-watering. The annual colosseum of televisual advertising – the US Super Bowl – boasts vast audiences, and hence has a cost of around US$5 million for a 30-second advertising spot. Each year, companies compete to outdo one another and be recognised as having the best commercials of the night. There is another look at TV advertising a little later in this chapter.

At the other end of the spectrum, the prevalence of regional TV and now the spread of the Internet have made this type of marketing accessible to any business that wants to use it. There are a wide range of approaches available, from the relatively indirect to the focused sales activation described previously.

Encourage donations/funding

The emotive power of video makes it an excellent tool for pulling on the audience's heart strings, and getting them to part with their money or time. I'm sure you're aware of the way that charities have used videos since the 1980s. These can also extend to Kickstarter and crowdfunding campaigns. Video's ability to simplify a message into a really compelling minute or so makes it excellent for this.

Introduce a business

As with encouraging funding, the ability to compress time and turn a 'who we are' PowerPoint presentation into a punchy 60-second promotion with music and branded graphics/colours makes video a useful tool to clarify exactly what your business does. The majority of websites that we've audited – over 1,000 thus far – aren't using video on their homepage. They rely on the visitor being able to grasp what the business does in the few brief seconds before they click elsewhere. It's a truism that people/businesses tend to market to themselves. As such, there is always far too much assumed knowledge, which makes websites impenetrable.

A video is a great way of capturing attention and explaining, in an accessible format, what the visitor should be looking for. This is why having a video on your homepage can improve click-through rates by up to 80%.[9]

This video can also be used in presentations, pitches, reception areas and for new joiners/potential recruits – anywhere you might want people to quickly understand, through compelling media, who you are and what you do.

Promote a product or service through explanation

"4x as many customers would rather watch a video about a product than read about it."

– Animoto, 2015[10]

Explaining succinctly what a product or service is or does is another effective use of video. Once again, most businesses communicating anything assume too much background knowledge (see box on page 72). In this instance, video can break down exactly what the product is and does, and build trust and understanding in an accessible package. This may be through an animation, which is effective when used to illustrate complex messaging, because of the ability to 'show and tell' at the same time as using accessible metaphors.

Another effective way to promote a service is through interview-led videos with experts, clients or users. These increase the audience's trust in the product by borrowing from the featured subject's standing: their expertise or experience. Interview-led films or 'talking heads' are useful because they are pretty much the cheapest videos to produce, and we find human faces innately intriguing.

Talking Heads

Interview-led or 'talking head' films are the backbone of corporate video. They are popular because they are cost-effective, easy to produce and an efficient way of communicating information. We naturally find fellow human faces interesting, so, in a sense, showing the people who are speaking is the best thing you can do as a filmmaker.

There are a number of ways that a simple talking head can be made more engaging, though. These include adding an animated element, dramatized scenes or relevant cutaway footage. Whatever you choose to overlay your interview, it's essential that they complement what is being said.

Get people excited

The moving nature of video makes it a great tool for exciting an audience about something. Admittedly, this could be an extension of promoting a product or service. However, it's distinct in that the method is less based on relaying information and explaining, and more focused on generating a positive emotion in the audience. One way of looking at it might be to say that explainer films engage the logical left side of the brain, while a film to get people excited targets the feeling, creative right side. These usually employ a stirring script and a voiceover with powerful music to do this. Both of these types of film, explainer and exciter, aim for the same outcome, though – getting the audience more engaged.

Increase brand awareness/tell a story

In reality, all the video content that companies share has the effect of building (or, unfortunately, sometimes damaging) their brand. Some videos are made specifically for this purpose, though. They may aim to align the business with a cause that matters to their target audience, or reflect on someone or something that they're interested in. It may extend to them wanting to share a story related to the company – the history or something that has inspired them.

Attract the best candidates

Video is an excellent way to illustrate relatively intangible things, such as a company's culture. Most people looking for a role at a new company will research what the job is about, beyond what is included in the job description. Video is a great way of sharing some of the things that make your company special.

In the hypercompetitive job market, more and more companies are having to compete with the likes of Facebook, Apple, Netflix, Microsoft, Amazon and Google for top technological talent. Simply put, all businesses are now technological businesses, so they have to recruit some of the brightest technological talent who'd initially think about going to one of the aforementioned 'big six'. This is particularly challenging given the absurdly deep pockets those companies have to hire staff.

The one area that other businesses can compete in is through an engaging, motivating and, crucially, well-communicated culture. Video can be invaluable in helping to build that culture through communicating what the concept of the brand means. This is where video can be invaluable – it allows you to communicate with your potential (and current) staff on an emotional level. One point to note is that, in the age of resources such as Glassdoor (which allows employees to rate employers for all to see), it's important that the offer and reality align.

Videos to promote and clarify a company's diversity and inclusion policies should be included here too.

Train your colleagues

Another type of internal communication that uses video is learning and development. The zero cost of distribution, and the ability to make changes and amendments to videos on an ongoing basis makes them useful for sharing information and training across a large organisation. Animation works well for information, and interactive video is good for training, because it allows viewers to choose responses and outcomes. The functionality of interactive video also allows for scorekeeping and sharing, which is a useful way of injecting a little competition into the learning process.

Beyond that, simply being able to show videos and then have people discuss them helps to increase the effectiveness of the learning.

Change behaviour

The external equivalent of internal training, making films to inform and change behaviour, is nearly as old as film itself; for example, the public-information films that were used to keep the population up to speed in the first half of the 20th century. The modern equivalents are usually produced by governments or charities.

Start a discussion/conversation

Video removes any unnecessary information and pauses. This condenses the amount of time it takes to share different viewpoints in an argument, which makes it useful for setting up a discussion. Such videos are usually played at the beginning of an online/offline discussion, or to change to another subject.

Record an event

The quality of an event film is, understandably, usually tied to the quality of the event itself. It's a useful way of encapsulating what happened, what was discussed or featured, and who was there. With some appropriate music and a dynamic edit, the video becomes a useful tool for promoting forthcoming events too.

But not everything – emotion vs information

All this having been said, there are some things that video isn't great at. Emotion and information exist in a balance in all films. Too much focus on emotion – with practically no information – and the film can feel superficial and lacking in substance (think of most fashion ads).

Too much information and not enough emotion, and the film will be dry, difficult to follow and impenetrable (some corporate reports embody this pitfall).

They should be like yin and yang. In every informative film you should have a bit of emotion, and in every emotive film you should have a bit of information (even if that is a basic narrative structure). Because of this, if you have lots and lots of information to get across, video might not be the best way to do it. You'll probably find it more effective to create a PDF document, use video to outline a few salient points and promote reading the PDF through a shorter, more engaging film.

YouTube's Content Structure
Hero, Hub and Hygiene/Help

In the same way that traditional channels have schedules and different types of show, so can your business. You don't necessarily need the full breadth of programmes that they have, but, to get you started thinking about the different categories that are available for building a resilient audience, YouTube has published a planning structure – hero, hub and hygiene – to cover the different ways that the online audience accesses video on the platform.

YouTube has realised that the user is drawn into an online video channel in one of two separate ways – they either see something that catches their eye, which gets them to click on it and watch it, or they type in a search term to find out about something that they are specifically looking for. Once on the channel, they should be encouraged to subscribe. From then on, they are sent notifications when the channel is updated with new material; this leads to the necessity of regular magazine-type content. These different types of content give rise to what they have termed *hero, hub* and *hygiene/help.*

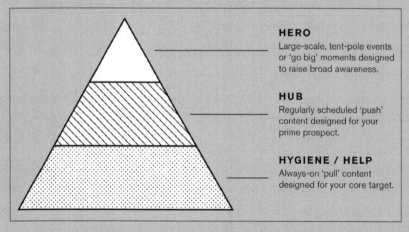

HERO
Large-scale, tent-pole events or 'go big' moments designed to raise broad awareness.

HUB
Regularly scheduled 'push' content designed for your prime prospect.

HYGIENE / HELP
Always-on 'pull' content designed for your core target.

Figure 2. The hero, hub and hygiene/help content structure

Hero

This is the really eye-catching, click-bait stuff. It's more akin to traditional TV advertising as a type. This is where you 'go big' to really raise awareness of your brand and the other content you're sharing. It's often 'chunked' or divided into shorter clips or images, and used as a promotion for the channel itself in banners on other sites. Because of this, its purpose is to catch the audience's eye with the concept, image or title as they browse elsewhere. They then click on the link and are drawn into watching the video, before being served the other content hosted on the channel.

Hub

This is the ongoing magazine-type material. This should be updated regularly with the goal of getting the audience to check back in to see what the latest show is. This is designed to be 'pushed' out to existing subscribers; this means that they will receive a notification when there is some new material for them to have a look at. They then click on this and revisit your channel.

Hygiene/Help

This is the content that people actually search for – how-tos, guides and instructions.

This type of content is designed to pull users into your channel through search results.

Initially, YouTube called this 'hygiene' because it's about things that people need to do. They since changed this to 'help', because that better reflects what it is/does.

By using the three different types to complement one another, it's possible to draw an ever-increasing number of subscribers into your channel – an initial goal of any channel operator. How this works can be seen in the diagram on the following page.

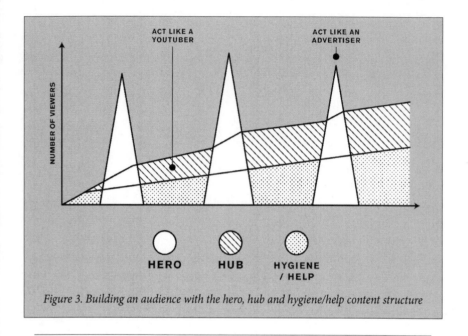

Figure 3. Building an audience with the hero, hub and hygiene/help content structure

Volvo Trucks - Case Study

It's easier to explain this content structure through examples, such as Volvo Trucks' YouTube channel. Volvo trucks sell... well, trucks, but, in order to do so, they've realised the value of speaking to a broad audience – not just their direct customers (the primary audience) but people who could influence their customers (the secondary audience).

To do this, Volvo have created a funnel, which makes use of the 'hero, hub and hygiene' content model. For the hero content they show eye-catching stunts (among other things), which act as the 'magazine cover'. The best example of this is their ad featuring Jean Claude van Damme doing the splits between two trucks. The hub content is comprised of the magazine-type shows that provide the central flow of the channel. Finally, the hygiene or help content features videos with subjects such as 'Why is Automation Good for Drivers?' and 'Explaining the Advantages of Platooning for Truck Enthusiasts, Truck Owners and Truck Fleet Buyers Interested in the Features of the Products.'

So far, the van Damme ad film has achieved 90 million YouTube views and 8 million shares, making it the most viewed automotive advert of all time. This is in addition to over 20,000 editorials and an earned media value of €126 million.

TV – Still the ultimate hero content

Despite the growth of YouTube, the boxset and recordable TV, television advertising isn't dead just yet. The majority of video is still watched 'down the line' on a TV set. While this amount is reducing, *if you can afford it*, TV advertising works very well in unison with online content. TV plays the role of the hero content in the preceding diagram – and drives additional viewers to your channel – but it's turbo charged in its effects. This is because TV significantly increases what is known in advertising circles as the 'fame' effect of your campaigns; i.e. getting people to talk about the campaign and about you. This is a powerful driver of positive brand association. It's a very effective way of launching further content online, by getting a large number of viewers hooked in, who then stay with you into the future.

TV advertising is expensive, and so it isn't accessible for everyone, but it can be very useful. This is backed up by analysis carried out by the Institute for Practitioners in Advertising (the IPA), which shows just how effective TV can be made when used in conjunction with online video. It found that TV commercials are still the most effective means of growing your brand's standing, but also that the most powerful campaigns, in terms of improving market share and through that your bottom line, are the ones that use the many different platforms that are available.[11]

'Big Rock' content

"What you're really seeking is to be trusted, to be heard, to be talked about, and to matter. And if we look at any brand that's succeeded, that is what they have done."

- Jason Miller, Content and Social Marketing Leader, LinkedIn Sales and Marketing Solutions EMEA[12]

The term 'Big Rock' content was initially coined by Jason Miller, LinkedIn's head of content. He describes it as a piece of content so substantial it allows you to, 'own the conversation'. This is the ultimate extension of Google's hero content (see previous box). Red Bull's 'Stratos Jump' is a perfect example of this; it's so audacious and the brand's ownership is so complete that it excludes anyone else from getting involved. However, this is maybe pushing the realms of possibility for 99% of brands. Nike's 'Breaking 2' was one of the standout pieces of content in 2017, where the brand got together three of the fastest marathon runners in an attempt to break the 2-hour barrier. The attempt created a large amount of support content, and earned interest from other online resources.[13]

A slightly more accessible example of this is Goldman Sachs *Talks at GS* series. These productions – reminiscent of TED talks in their approach and quality – feature presidents, actors, and business and charity founders, who are some of the most interesting thinkers and personalities of our time. The interviews are up to 20 to 30 minutes in length, which means that there is loads of content that can be repurposed into shorter outputs to be shared elsewhere. The channel sets the bank up as a powerhouse for global business and financial success, and has earned over 30 million views on YouTube so far.

Whatever you decide to make your 'Big Rock', there are a couple of things to keep in mind:

» Make it really big and really desirable. It needs to be audacious and eye-catching enough for your audience to share their personal details with you to get involved. This may just be an email address, but it could be so significant that they will actually pay for it. Whatever the goal – make it big.

» Consider two points: What conversation do you want to own? What is the number-one question on your audience's minds? Where do these two questions intersect? They may well not, in which case you need to think about how you can transpose the two without compromising too much. This is where you should place your 'Big Rock'.

Once you've made the investment in your 'Big Rock', you can repurpose parts of the output again and again. You can use these smaller pieces of content to drive engagement with the central story. This can, in turn, massively increase your return on the original investment.

Making the sale

We looked at what makes video such an effective tool for corporate communicators in Chapter 1. It's understood by psychologists that we make the decision to act emotionally, but then we back up this decision logically. For example, in making the decision to buy a new car, an individual might choose a certain model because she likes the way it looks, the colour and how sitting in it makes her feel, but would then rationalise this decision through the great fuel economy, financing and crash-safety rating. Because of this, it's important that the content you produce plays to both sides of your audience's reasons for taking action. This is why really effective marketing campaigns combine two distinct angles: emotion-driving brand building and logically appealing sales activation. Let's look at these two in a little more depth.

Brand building

> *"Video advertising, both on and offline, is the most effective brand-building form."*
> – IPA Media in Focus Report[14]

Brand building focuses on creating a positive emotional connection with the brand. These are the associations and beliefs that make the customer more likely to buy from one brand over another. This requires repeated exposure to consistent messaging, slowly building a compelling image of what that brand represents, produces and stands for. While this takes time to achieve, the effects are deep seated in the audience and lead to the best long-term effects.

The consistent nature of brand building has the additional benefit of creating followers among people who might not be in the market for the brand's product at the time of exposure. This is important because the audience aren't looking to purchase for the majority of the time. As discussed in Chapter 1, video's emotive power makes it an extremely valuable tool because it's so much more memorable.

Creating raving fans/evangelists

Brand building also gives you the opportunity to build your customers into advocates for your brand. Each interaction they have with you will make them feel either more or less positive about you. Your product, delivery and customer service all play into this, but so does your content strategy. With everyone now having the power to communicate at their fingertips, you should be looking to build each of your customers to the point where they will do your marketing for you.

This is the most effective form of marketing available – the challenge is that it's hard to do at scale. On the one hand, this may be writing positive reviews, defending what you do in chat rooms or simply recommending your product to their friends. This may also be by retweeting a video you've created, because it resonates so strongly with them, or re-editing and sharing some content that you created for that purpose. Whatever it is, you must build their brand loyalty and then make it as easy as possible for them to do this for you. The process from sceptics, through customers and into advocates is shown here:

Figure 4: The audience attitude continuum

All of the content that you share should increase the positive perception of your brand in your audience's eyes. The most positive 'raving fans' love your brand so much that they practically can't stop going on about it. This is your goal for as many of your audience/customers as possible.

Sales activation

Sales activation is targeted at those who are likely to buy in the very near future. This aims to encourage the buyer to make a purchase and aims to make the purchase as frictionless as possible. These include discounts, vouchers, special offers, unique experiences and seasonal sales, and are far more targeted at the individual than the broader nature of brand-building content. The more bought into your brand your audience are, the more effective this type of content will be. This is a great opportunity to further strengthen your follower base by offering them favourable terms if they are a subscriber to your channel.

Sales-activation messages take advantage of the positive brand associations that you've built up in other areas and with your other communications. The effects of sales-activation approaches cause a short-term spike in purchasing intent, which drops off rapidly. Because of this, the two approaches are best used hand in hand, with the IPA's 2017 Media in Focus report recommending a 60:40 split of brand building to activation as the optimum ratio.[15]

In Summary: What You Should Be Broadcasting

In this chapter, we've looked at how increases in the mobility of the online audience means that they are now in charge. This means that the type of content they are looking for has to have value to them – they will no longer engage with material that doesn't. This has led to a significant rise in the popularity of branded content or content marketing.

A useful way to think about the different types of value content can provide is with the mnemonic TRUE: it should be timely, relevant, useful and/or entertaining for your target audience.

Businesses can use video in a wide range of different ways:

- ✓ To boost sales
- ✓ To encourage donations/funding
- ✓ To introduce a business
- ✓ To promote a product or service through explanation
- ✓ To get people excited
- ✓ To increase brand awareness/tell a story
- ✓ To attract the best candidates
- ✓ To train your colleagues
- ✓ To change behaviour
- ✓ To start a discussion/conversation
- ✓ To record an event

If you've got a large amount of information to share, it might be better to create a PDF or website, and then use video to generate interest in it.

YouTube have developed a useful strategy for creating videos that fit into how they have seen people using their platform. This strategy splits content into these three categories:

Hero content is eye-catching, and draws the viewer on to the channel while they are browsing elsewhere. This is akin to traditional commercial advertising – TV ads are still the king of hero content.

Hub content is ongoing magazine-type content, which is produced regularly to be pushed out to the viewer through notifications, once they have subscribed to see further material. This is the core of the channel.

Hygiene/help content is helpful, how-to type content for which people might enter the terms into a search engine. This then draws them into the rest of the channel, where they are compelled to subscribe.

'**Big Rock**' **content** is a type of hero content of such scale and ambition that it allows you to own the conversation around it. It also generates lots and lots of complementary content, which can be shared to promote it. Nike's 'Breaking 2' is a good example of this.

All of the content that you share will build trust and affinity with your brand among its audience. Once you've built enough trust, you can start to recommend your products or to share special offers that more explicitly drive the audience towards the sale. *Do not* do this too early, as you run the risk of burying the trust you're trying to build.

In the next chapter, we'll look at the importance of trust, purpose and backing up words with actions. We'll look at the benefits that this can hold for your company and our world.

CHAPTER 4

USING PURPOSE AS THE CORNERSTONE FOR YOUR CONTENT

In the first few chapters of this book, we looked at why video is such a powerful tool, and how advances in technology have put that power into all of our hands. We also looked at how businesses need to think about the video they share as another product – it's a key element of their value proposition to their customers.

In this chapter, I want to look at the *other effects* of the prevalence of connected devices and video technology. We'll look at why *business purpose* is such a valuable resource for communicators like you. Through that, I'll show you why making the world a cleaner, greener, fairer place is good for business.

This chapter covers five main points:

1. Why we're living in the 'Age of Transparency'
2. Building trust in the era of 'fake news'
3. The purpose of purpose in the content of content
4. "With great power comes great responsibility"
5. Actions matter more than words

The 'Age of Transparency'

The technological evolutions covered in the previous chapters have changed the nature of communication: it's no longer simply the few *with* the means broadcasting to the masses *without*. Communication is now omnidirectional: everyone is broadcasting, commenting on and sharing each other's messages. This environment presents significant challenges for corporate communicators in particular – consistency of message is key. Out of sight is no longer out of mind. In the globalised world, eyes and cameras are everywhere. Blue-chip megaliths can lose billions in market capitalisation from a single incident, with their reaction magnified to the world by omnipresent smartphones. This 'all-seeing eye' has illuminated areas that were closed off before. We've become more familiar with the workings of authority. With this familiarity, contempt has crept in, which has led to a general crisis of trust.

Scandals in almost every field – for example, sexual harassment/#MeToo, politics, corporate malpractice, police mistreatment (e.g. Black Lives Matter) and hacked answerphones – have led to historically low trust ratings for the traditional pillars of power.[1] Traditional broadcasters are suffering from an onslaught of new media and a resurgent, divisive political movement intent on dismissing discourse; this increases and aims to capitalise on the trust gap.

Set against this backdrop, it's not surprising that trust has become a, if not *the*, watchword of business communications. Every business function – from product launches to temporary-staff induction – has to be performed as if the world is watching, because, frankly, it could be.

There is now a constant check on all of your operations and communications. Would-be citizen journalists armed with camera phones are everywhere, as United Airlines found out in April 2017 when their security staff forcibly removed a passenger from a flight at Chicago O'Hare Airport. What was once an anecdote shared among friends now has the potential to become global news, aided by the power of moving image.

Put a foot wrong and whistle-blowers – both internal and external – have the means to call you out in potentially ruinous ways. This phenomenon has made various commentators describe the modern age as the 'Age of Transparency'.[2]

Lost in Translation – Eastern vs Western Interpretations of Trust

One of the major challenges for global businesses in growing trust internationally is that the Western and Eastern definitions of trust are so drastically different. In the West, it's believed that you gain trust by acting with integrity and demonstrating your competence, usually over time. In the East, trust is something that belongs to your relations, or the people that live in your town or village. The Western version is earned; the Eastern version arises from shared belonging. This makes scaling trust in the East rather more challenging.

This also explains the success different social media platforms have in each market (notwithstanding the fact that Facebook is banned in China). Facebook in the West effectively allows you to share information with everyone on the platform. WeChat in China is essentially a large collection of private groups where information is shared between members who already know each other. These conflicting definitions must be considered for any business looking to succeed with its global communications strategy.

Building Trust in the Era of 'Fake News'*

"Trust is built on authenticity."

– Brian Tracy

Beyond the obvious complexities of operating in this 'Age of Transparency' lie the challenges of dealing with 'fake news'. The ability to broadcast has been used by some to share their own 'alternative facts'.

---

* Have faith. All new technology takes a little time for people to understand and use effectively. Think of the men with red flags running in front of early cars to warn pedestrians, or cell phones ringing all the time before society discovered the vibrate function. We're living through an unprecedented period of technological advancement, so it's unsurprising that there will be some growing pains. As I write, some of our brightest minds are working on solutions to these challenges.

While this has impacted traditional media and governments more significantly, it's still a key concern for those in business communications.

Credibility is essential. This is particularly true given that, according to PR giant Edelman's *Annual Global Trust Survey*, 69% of those questioned believe that the most important role for the CEO is to make sure that their company is trusted.[3] It's essential to build and maximise the trust of your audience – your employees, your customers and your shareholders – but it can feel like you're swimming against the current. So, how can your communications help you to do that?

Make it about the audience

The most valuable thing you can do to make your content resonate, is to make sure that it's right for your audience. They know themselves better than anyone, so they instinctively know what rings true and what feels false.

Be mindful about where your content appears

Be careful where you allow your brand to feature online. The whole online environment isn't as low trust as it might appear at first. There are trusted pockets. It's important to seek these out, and to avoid sharing content where it might appear alongside other material you wouldn't want to endorse.

Act with humility

Be prepared to share the challenges as well as the successes. The greatest stories, with the greatest heroes, aren't defined by unremitting success. They are made great through adversity. Share your adversity; you'll enrich your narrative and the audience will come with you.

Be transparent

Brands have been forced to deal directly with complaints and criticism of their online profiles for several years now. Those who have taken an ostrich-like head-in-the-sand approach have suffered significantly as a result. It isn't an option to not engage, and yet very few, if any, companies have actively welcomed that negative feedback at a deep level and used it to improve themselves. There are, of course, huge challenges in operating a global business. The audience understand this. As with the previous point, put your hands up and explain that you don't have all the answers, but that you're doing your best. They'll love you for it.

> *"Being transparent is what gives our business its most important asset – trust. At a time when there is a crisis of trust in many institutions across the world, there has never been a more important time for business to play a leading role in restoring it."*
> – Paul Polman, CEO, Unilever[4]

Be consistent

You'll gain the trust of your customers through delivering quality and value in both the content you produce and your products/services. Consumers like to know what they're going to get, and will prefer to go with something that they know will be a 7/10, rather than shooting for a 9/10 and risking ending up with a 3/10. This desire for the 'known' explains the success of business chains to a large degree.

Deliver on what you promise

Don't say anything that you can't back up with action, again and again. There will be more on this shortly.

Have a higher purpose

purpose

ˈpərpəs/

noun

"A person, object or organisation's reason for being."[5]

For organisations, these are aspirational by their nature, grounded in humanity and go beyond the profit motive. A business's purpose is often referred to as its 'North Star' – an unattainable, guiding light, against which all activities are measured. It provides clarity for all the decision-making in the business, from the significantly strategic to the day-to-day tactical.

"Purpose is a long-term, forward-looking intention to accomplish aims that are both meaningful to the self and of consequence to the world beyond."[6]

– Bill Damon, Director, Stanford Center on Adolescence

Purpose has come to be referred to as the 'Why?' for a business, as outlined by Simon Sinek in his excellent book *Start with the Why.*[7] It should clearly articulate the stance of the business, allowing everyone who comes into contact with it to identify whether it aligns with their own value structure and aspirations. As this alignment grows, it graduates to a state that stakeholders are able to describe as 'belonging'. This desire to belong to a tribe answers a base yearning within us all. Many of the most successful businesses of our time – Zappos, Ben and Jerry's, and Apple – have grown through the successful propagation of a tribal belonging among their staff and customers. This is only possible through a powerfully articulated, clear purpose.

This success has led to purpose becoming en vogue for much of the business world. It's no longer enough to exist to 'maximise shareholder value'. In the post-2007 world, purpose- and cause-driven business is more important than ever.

The Purpose of Purpose in the Content of your Content

Why am I suddenly talking about purpose in a book about video? This is because the fact that it resonates so strongly with your audience makes it a valuable resource when looking for content to broadcast or campaigns to run. This doesn't mean that all the content you create should suddenly be about charities or that it should be about 'do-gooding'. It also doesn't mean that all your content needs to be about your corporate purpose. It means that *all the content that you create should have a tangential relevance to your 'Why?' as a business.* This will provide an underlying coherence to your content at the same time as reinforcing your brand identity. It's a step towards your purpose being about actions, rather than just words.

While purpose is extremely valuable to corporate communicators, it must be ingrained in your way of doing business. It isn't enough to simply talk about it: it must become part of your DNA. Your customers and employees will thank you for it, as will your shareholders in due course, so everyone ends up happy.

Purpose and the Zuckerberg generation

Purpose has become particularly important given the evolutions in employment patterns in the current century. Speak to most employers, and they will complain that today's youthful workforce has become less loyal and more flighty, but the facts don't entirely bear this out.*[8]

What has happened, without question, is a shift in what the workforce want from a job. Millennials have seen their contemporaries overturn convention and earn billions as the creators of global technology brands. From Ed Sheeran and Justin Bieber to Malala Yousafzai, they have seen how a compelling story can pluck anyone from obscurity and plaster them across the global stage. They mainline videos that show them what is happening in the world – *their* world – and how they can and must play a role in shaping it. 'Shape the world' is what they plan to do.

Young people naturally find it easier to pick up new things (which is just as well). This has meant that they have been disproportionately empowered by the *Technological Revolution* (see Chapter 2). This is upending traditional power structures. They know they have this power, and want to know what the brands they interact with – as their suppliers, employers and broadcasters – will do for them. Young people no longer *live to work*, they *work to live*. Work is something that the modern employee does as a part of their life. They expect to live the life of their choosing, which means that all employment is viewed through a 'What's in it for me?' prism. Each job has to be a stepping stone or stamp to their career passport, enhancing their skills and experience to enable the next leap onwards. Millennials have never known a world not negatively affected by human impact.

---

* According to LinkedIn, millennials – those born between 1982 and 2000 (and among the 500 million who use the platform) – change job four times on average in their first ten years in the workplace. There is disagreement over whether this represents a significant departure from previous generations. A US Bureau of Labor Statistics study of the baby-boomer generation (see the following reference) found that they had held an average of 11.7 jobs between the ages of 18 and 48. This is certainly more than the baby boomers' grandparents would have had at the turn of the 20th century.

Climate change, the 'plastification' of the oceans, mass extinction and social inequality all play on their minds. They want the businesses that they have a relationship with to be part of the solution to these problems. This explains why business purpose is so specifically important to them, particularly when choosing an employer.

They believe that business can be a genuine force for good in the world. Of the 7,900 young people surveyed as part of the *Deloitte Global Millennial Survey 2017*, 76% view 'business' positively and believe that it has a positive influence on society.[9] This rose to 89% among those considered to be 'hyperconnected millennials'; i.e. those identified as being highly digitally connected compared to the average in their own countries. *Nine out of ten of the most influential millennials believe that business has a positive influence on society.* As the guardians of big business, you should seize this opportunity and build on it.

Why should this matter to you?

This matters because the millennials are becoming the most powerful generation in history. They are the largest generation (92 million in the US), surpassing the baby boomers (77 million US), and are entering the workplace and their prime earning/spending years. By 2025 they will make up 75% of the global workforce. They already control US$2.7 trillion in annual expenditure. In the West, over time, they will inherit the wealth of their baby-boomer parents, much of which has been protected and built by final-salary pensions and significant real-estate-asset inflation. *They are the future of business and our planet.*

Young people want purpose, belonging and ownership of the brands they interact with – your brand. They want to take part. They have grown up surrounded by social media and technology in the post-9/11 world. Having a purpose to work towards makes them more-engaged employees, more-loyal customers and more-active advocates for your brand. They want you to be part of the solution, and they want you to be the enabler.

For employees, the ability to take part in charitable causes at work leads to an increase in loyalty. Deloittes' aforementioned survey found that of the 54% of millennials who were provided with the opportunity to contribute to good causes or charities, 35% stayed in their job for 5 years or more (vs

24% without the opportunity).[10] They were also more positive about the role of business in the world and more optimistic about the social situation generally.

It's not just employee engagement that makes this a good area for your business to get involved in. There's also the direct-profit motive. Around *89%* of millennial consumers have said there is a strong likelihood they would buy from companies that support solutions to particular social issues, and *91%* said that this fact would increase their trust in the business.[11] This would explain why market-research firm Nielsen identified that, in the financial year 2015, sales of consumer goods from brands with a demonstrated commitment to sustainability grew more than 4% globally, while those without grew less than 1%.[*;12]

Business steps up

*"We cannot close our eyes to the challenges the world faces.
Business must make an explicit positive contribution to
addressing them. Business has to change."*

– Paul Polman, CEO, Unilever[13]

The last few years have seen a concerning increase in the amount of political division in the Western world. Much of this has been driven by people who put their personal political advancement ahead of the harmony of their people. As a reaction to this, we're already starting to see visionary businesses take more-inclusive political stances. Gone are the days when all business sat on the sidelines, unwilling to take a stand for fear of alienating potential customers. Take a stand and your audience know where they stand – it gives them the opportunity to belong.

At the 2017 Super Bowl, a number of the commercials had a political, pro-inclusivity sentiment to them. There have been significant responses to many of the policies laid out by Donald Trump as president. These range from the condemnation of his 'Muslim ban' to consternation at his decision to withdraw the US from the 2015 Paris Climate Agreement, which drew heated statements from the CEOs of many of the Fortune 500 companies.

---

* *The Nielsen study looked at over 1,300 brands in 13 categories in an average of 13 countries.*

Jigsaw Gets Political - Case Study

In 2017, UK fashion brand Jigsaw decided to take a stand against rising anti-immigration sentiment in the UK. They worked with genealogy-testing website Ancestry.co.uk to understand the history of immigration within the business, before creating their 'Love Immigration' campaign.

"Fashion doesn't operate in a bubble. We could just talk about clothes, but with what is going on around us it seems hypocritical and superficial to not accept the debt we owe to immigration in its broadest sense. Be it people, cloth, the stone floors in our shops, [or] the film to shoot our campaigns. We are all part of a vibrant, tolerant, global Britain. These are things we believe in as a brand."[14] - Peter Ruis, Jigsaw's CEO

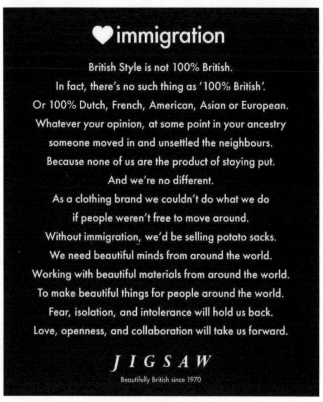

Figure 5. Jigsaw's Instagram post

The campaign won *Marketing Week's* Best Campaign of 2017, with 81% of the vote.[15] For a long time in the UK, as with much of the Western world, there has been an absence of politicians making the positive case for immigration for fear of damaging their electability. It's a telling illustration of the way that power is shifting that it has needed a business to take up the mantle and use its marketing budget to promote decency.

Patagonia Gets Immersive - Case Study

Across 'the Pond', outdoors company Patagonia responded to the Trump administration's decision to reduce the size of the Bears Ears and Grand Staircase Escalante national monuments by taking a stance against it. They created a stunning VR/360° video website called *Defend Bears Ears* to allow visitors to experience the natural beauty and grandeur of the site. Having impressed and engaged them, the site then urges its visitors to take action against the decision.

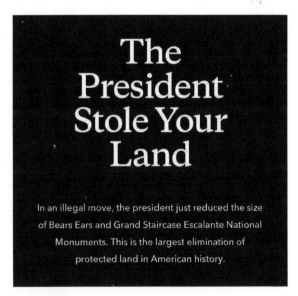

Figure 6. Patagonia's Instagram post

This is an excellent example of using the functionality of technology – in this case fully immersive 360° video and sound – to aid the aim of the content. By immersing the viewer in the experience, Patagonia is able to relocate the viewer to the parks.

They cross promoted this on their blog – the *Cleanest Line* – telling visitors that "The President Stole Your Land". Not only did this raise awareness of the event and what was at stake, it also added significantly to the company's bottom line. *Go to http://bearsears.patagonia.com to experience it.**

> *"78% of Americans believe it's important for companies to stand up for important social justice issues. This rises to 90% among African Americans."*
>
> – Cone Communications[16]

UK-based, certified, purpose-driven businesses (B-Corps) grew 28 times faster than the national average in the financial year 2018.[17]

> *"With great power comes great responsibility."*
>
> – French National Convention, 1793 via *Spiderman*, 1953

Business is the most powerful man-made force in the modern world. It affects every home and influences every government. It has been the engine for financial advancement that has reduced inequality globally and reduced the number of people living in extreme poverty (by the current metric of those living on less than US$1.90/day) by 74.1% in 25 years, according to the World Bank.**[18] It improves and enables lives, imbuing them with purpose and meaning on a global scale. We couldn't have advanced beyond the Middle Ages without it. This power is greater than it has ever been. Big business has won big on the back of global shifts in power – now it has to give back.

---

*As with all the links mentioned in this book, you can find it at www.newfirebook.com/links

**A total of 1.9 billion people (or 37.1% of the global population) lived on less than $1.90 a day in 1990, compared to a projected 702 million (9.6%) in 2015.

Globalisation is here to stay – business must make it work

Business is in a strong position to do this. You have a good start – the generation of the future believe business to be a force for good.

Business must now step forwards and take responsibility for the world it exists in and draws profits from. There have been winners and losers as the world's economy has globalised. Despite recent nationalist, isolationist political upsets in the Western world, as US Secretary of State, John Kerry said, "You cannot put the globalisation genie back in the bottle", to fight against it is to lose ground and compound the damage.[19] Environmentally too, 200 years of ever-increasing prosperity has caused damage. Business has benefitted, so business needs to take ownership of some of the challenges that have been created. It's the most potent weapon that mankind has to resolve these issues.

In *Thank You for Being Late*, Thomas Friedman quotes an excellent metaphor to describe how to survive in the ever-accelerating world, which is from a blog by Anna Levesque, a former Canadian freestyle kayaker and Olympic bronze medallist.[20] She knows her stuff; she has more than 15 years of experience as an international competitor, instructor and guide. According to Levesque, newbies who are confronted by white water for the first time tend to freak out and stick their oar in the fast-flowing water, trying to slow down or stop. This is a completely natural reaction, but it has the effect of destabilising the canoe, often making it capsize. The best policy to survive in a fast-flowing stream is to try to paddle faster than the water around you.[21]

That is, to survive in the ever-accelerating world, we need to learn to evolve and move faster than we ever have in the past. The sad thing about much of the political isolationism and nationalism is that it's the result of populations wanting to plunge their oar into the ever-accelerating stream, trying to get back to when the water was a little more sedate. Unfortunately, this will lead to the very opposite of what most of these people want. Business has benefitted from the forces that have carried us here; now it must help to stabilise the boat, and assist those who have been left behind.[22]

While the challenges we face maybe more significant than they have ever been, so is our ability to overcome them.

United Nations (UN) Sustainable Development Goals (SDGs)

The UN SDGs or 2030 Agenda aims to tackle some of the most pressing challenges humanity faces. These include no poverty (Goal 1); gender equality (Goal 5); and peace, justice and strong institutions (Goal 16). They grew out of the Millennium Development Goals, which were set out by the UN to mark the millennium positively. According to the Business and Sustainable Development Commission's *Better Business, Better World Report*, the SDGs could generate an additional US$12 trillion in additional business opportunities each year.[23] They are an excellent place to look for opportunities to grow your bottom line while building trust with consumers.

Long-termism pays

*"Economic performance is not the only responsibility of a business…
without responsibility, power degenerates into non-performance.
So the demand for socially responsible organizations will not go away;
rather, it will widen."* [24]

– Peter Drucker

The great global recession of 2008 has led to the very nature of capitalism being questioned. In the public consciousness, much of the blame for the crisis fell at the feet of bankers, lenders and businesspeople focusing too much on short-term returns and not enough on long-term resilience. The disenchantment with the current environment has even extended to the nature of business and capitalism being questioned. In order to continue to function with the public's assent, business needs to take steps (and be seen to take steps) to address their long-term impact, and win back the trust that has waned in recent years.

As McKinsey shows in its Corporate Horizon index, taking a long-term approach leads to better performance across five key factors, including earnings, job creation, market capitalisation and profit. It tracked 615 large and middle-capitalisation (mid-cap) US publicly listed companies from 2001 to 2015, based on patterns of growth, investment, earnings quality and earnings management. This then allowed it to assess each company's relative performance based on its behaviour.

McKinsey found that, between 2001 and 2014, the revenue of long-termist firms grew on average by 47% more than the revenue of the other firms in its study. The economic profit of these long-termist firms grew 81% more on average. These companies also added 12,000 more jobs in the 15 years to 2015. McKinsey found that the potential value unlocked by companies taking a longer-term approach was worth more than US$1 trillion in forgone US gross domestic product (GDP) over the decade to 2015.[25]

There are still challenges – 87% of executives and directors say that demonstrating strong financial performance in 2 years or less is their most pressing priority.[26] That said, the extent to which this movement has become a mainstream way of thinking is reflected on by BlackRock chairman, Larry Fink:

"Society is demanding that companies, both public and private, serve a social purpose. To prosper over time, every company must not only deliver financial performance, but also show how it makes a positive contribution to society. Companies must benefit all of their stakeholders, including shareholders, employees, customers, and the communities in which they operate.

"Companies must ask themselves: What role do we play in the community? How are we managing our impact on the environment? Are we working to create a diverse workforce? Are we adapting to technological change? [...] Today, our clients – who are your company's owners – are asking you to demonstrate the leadership and clarity that will drive not only their own investment returns, but also the prosperity and security of their fellow citizens." [27]

With a global population of over 9 billion people expected by the year 2050, in order to survive, business must be driving the solution to the challenges that it will bring. A failure to do this will lead to a lack of any future market in which to sell your goods and services. This isn't a 'tree hugging' environmentalist plea, this is a reality we must all grasp.

By 2050, there will be no such thing as 'sustainable' business; there will be only business.

Unilever - Long-termist - Case Study

Paul Polman took over as CEO at Unilever in 2009. Since then, he has shifted the business strategy towards long-term, resilient returns. He saw the obsession with short-term returns as the root of the mess that the world had ended up in, post 2008. He created a strategy to turn this on its head, and generated a longer-term plan. He stopped quarterly reporting, and increased investment in research and development (R&D), capital expenditure, and information technology (IT). The share price dropped 8% on the day he unveiled his plan, but, over time, he was able to explain the benefits to shareholders.

"Transparency builds trust ... We spent a disproportionate amount of time explaining why a more socially responsible business model is actually also a better model for the shareholders longer term."[28]

– Paul Polman, CEO, Unilever

Polman's defining initiative was the 10-year *Unilever Sustainable Living Plan*, which is based on the UN SDGs (see box on page 112).

This has three central pillars:

1. Taking action to improve the health of 1 billion people by 2020. This includes providing safe drinking water and sanitation, and improving self-esteem and skin health, among other things.

2. Reducing the environmental impact of making and using their products by half by 2030, while growing the business. This includes

reducing greenhouse gases despite growth, reducing water use and promoting the circular economy (designing packaging and workflows so that they can be reused).

3. Enhancing the livelihoods of millions of people as they grow, by promoting fairness in the workplace and increasing opportunities for women.[29]

Hitting these targets will have significant benefits for the people they touch. They are also really good business for Unilever. In May 2018, the company announced that its 26 'sustainable living' brands had grown 46% faster than the rest of the business. It classifies these brands as being further down the track to hitting the company's ambitious sustainability targets.[30]

"87% of Americans would purchase a product because that company stood up for or advocated for an issue that they care about."
– Cone Communications[31]

Actions Matter More than Words

"[Cause marketing] is no longer a competitive differentiator unless it is also accompanied by a genuine effort on the part of companies to demonstrate how their efforts were making a real impact on achieving results."
– Cone Communications[32]

Cone Communications has been running an annual study on the efficacy of cause-related marketing. It found that this is no longer a differentiator, unless it's also accompanied by a genuine effort by the companies to demonstrate they are achieving an actual impact. Unfortunately, this shows it's not enough to simply talk about the great projects that you're putting money into. Audiences are far more likely to talk about what a brand did than what they said. This means that, in order to make taking a more conscientious approach work for you, you actually need to get your hands dirty. You must 'live your purpose'. It should shine through in everything that you do. Failure to do this leads to a perceived lack of authenticity in the eyes of your stakeholders, which, thanks to social media, will do disproportionate damage to your brand.

It's also important to get intimately involved in the causes that you wish to benefit in order to avoid the charge of 'jumping on the bandwagon', as Pepsi found with their Kendall Jenner protestors spot...

Getting it Wrong - Pepsi and Kendall Jenner

Whatever cause you decide to get involved in, it's essential that your brand has an authentic attachment to the cause. This cannot just be lip service. It's also extremely important that you understand the nuances of the issue and don't trivialise it through superficial understanding. Pepsi's Kendall Jenner commercial shows her giving cans of Pepsi to police officers, seemingly with a view to reducing tensions at a *Black Lives Matter* protest. The idea that Jenner, who is white, could turn up and solve the situation with a can of soda was seen as extremely insulting and out of touch. Social media did the rest, culminating in the 18-year-old model sharing a video with her crying and begging the forgiveness of the masses.

It might be tempting to move away from cause-related marketing as a result. The key point here is that if you're going to take this route, which you should, you need to get involved at the root, make a difference and then tell that story. It is not acceptable to simply say, from a disconnected position, that you 'believe' in good causes. It is necessary to actually become involved in them, to understand them and to benefit them – to use your considerable might to work towards a solution, no matter how small the step you enable might be.

Greenwashing

greenwash

/'griːnwɒʃ/

noun

"Disinformation disseminated by an organisation so as to present an environmentally responsible public image."[33]

Greenwashing is marketing that intentionally overemphasises the green credentials of a business activity, while downplaying the actual negative impact. As a term, it was first used by Jay Westervelt in an essay criticising the hotel industry for their habit of leaving cards in their bathrooms asking their guests to reduce the amount of washing that is done by not leaving their towels on the floor, from where they would have to be washed. Westervelt showed that, far from being motivated by the environment, the hoteliers were in fact motivated by the reduced costs it would incur, thereby increasing their profits.[34]

> It isn't a new thing though, in 1969 alone, public utilities spent more than US$300 million on advertising their green credentials – more than eight times what they spent on the anti-pollution research they were touting in those ads.

Greenwashing became more elaborate through the 1970s and 1980s, to the extent that in 1990, on Earth Day 20, one-quarter of all goods launched in the US were marketed as being, *recyclable, ozone friendly and compostable.*[35] In 1985, Chevron launched their *People Do* series, which was aimed at those who were societally conscious and hostile to the company. The ads featured bears, eagles and animals, and underlined how hard the company's people were working to protect wildlife during their work. These ran for 15 years and became a textbook case of how successful greenwashing can be, leading to a 10% jump in sales and a 22% jump among the hostile audience target group.[36]

Greenwashing in the current 'post-truth' age is alive and well. The bottled-water industry, for example, leans heavily on imagery of the natural world in its marketing, and trumpets the reduction in plastic used in its bottles, while its products continue to have a severely negative ecological impact. Only 31% of plastic bottles consumed in the US are recycled.[37] With so much demand for 'green' products (72% of millennials will pay more for environmentally sustainable products),[38] it's not surprising that businesses are keen to stress their credentials.

In Summary: Using Purpose as the Cornerstone for your Content

In this chapter, we've looked at the value of purpose to content producers. Taking steps to fix the world can be useful beyond leaving the planet in a reasonable state for our children. It can make your content far more effective, consistent and valuable.

There are five main points you need to consider.

1. Why we're living in the 'Age of Transparency'

Technological advances have shone a light behind the scenes of almost every established institution. This has coincided with a general degeneration in the level of deference to those bodies. Now that everyone has a smartphone, they have the ability to call businesses out when they step out of line. Repeated scandals have led to a crisis of trust.

2. Building trust in the era of 'fake news'

Further amplifying this crisis is the reality that the factual truth itself is being questioned. This makes it even more challenging for businesses to rebuild trust, which is the number-one element in the sales/recruitment process. There are a number of ways that your communications can help you rebuild this trust, though. They are being mindful of where your content is being shared, acting with humility, being consistent and doing what you say you'll do. Don't lie and don't spin.

3.   The purpose of purpose in the content of content

Having a clearly defined and communicated business purpose is like having a North Star for the business. It's a significant asset for a number of reasons. These include better staff retention, better audience engagement and a more loyal customer base.

People care about purpose. This makes it a great area to look to for things to broadcast about. If you anchor all of the content that you produce in your purpose, you'll ensure that there is consistency of message.

Your content doesn't need to be all about your purpose directly, but you should be able to draw a direct line between it and the videos you make.

4.   "With great power comes great responsibility"

Business is the most powerful man-made force in the world. This world faces a number of significant challenges. Business has benefitted greatly from globalisation, and it has played its role in bringing about climate change. *Now is the time to stand up and be a part of the solution.* It may help the world avoid a cataclysm. It makes excellent business sense and gives the opportunity for a lot of excellent content. Your audience are less cynical than you think about business being part of the solution. You must grasp this opportunity and rebuild their trust.

5.   Actions matter more than words

Content has to be created around genuine initiatives. You must 'walk the walk' before you 'talk the talk'. *You must 'live your purpose'.* Failure to do this will lead to significant brand damage online. Don't be guilty of greenwashing.

In the next part of the book, we'll look at the different stages of video production and the points that you need to know to commission better video.

PART 2

MAKING IT HAPPEN
A COMMISSIONERS GUIDE

Overview

In Part 1, we looked at how advances in technology have made it possible for us all to operate our own media channel. This represents an excellent opportunity for brands to build their value by shifting their marketing strategy to operate like a broadcaster. In this next part of the book, we'll look at how you do this. By now, you'll hopefully understand how the role of video has changed for corporate communicators. You'll have been given some ideas about *what* you might choose to broadcast about. We'll now look at *how* to do it.

You should read this because a better understanding of the process will make you a better user, commissioner and/or producer of video content. There are literally thousands of books and YouTube videos on how to make videos, so I'm not going to go over that here. This part is for commissioners, working within large corporates, who will have the ability to work with technicians to get the actual work done, whether that is using internal resources – such as staff filmmakers, contract staff or freelancers – or going externally to production companies, agencies or digital freelancer networks.

Before 2005, people working the production industry liked to paint the production process as a dark art. Requests from inexperienced clients could be dismissed or capitalised on with a 'that's not possible'/'that's going to cost a lot' suck of the teeth and a tilt of the head. This is no longer the case. The tools are more accessible than ever before. The next part will help you get the most out of working with them.

The chapters are as follows:

» Chapter 5: The Video-Production Process (An Overview)

» Chapter 6: Writing a Winning Brief

» Chapter 7: Defining Your Target Audience

» Chapter 8: Setting the Budget

» Chapter 9: Getting the Right Creative Idea

» Chapter 10: How to Find and Tell Great Stories

» Chapter 11: Data

» Chapter 12: The Optimal Length for Online Videos

» Chapter 13: Choosing the Right Partner – Agency/Internal/ Freelance

» Chapter 14: Distribution Planning

» Chapter 15: The Ten Commandments For Creating Better Video

CHAPTER 5

THE VIDEO-PRODUCTION PROCESS

This chapter is split into two sections. Section one deals with the different stages in the production. Section two gives an overview of some of the different roles that work together to deliver it.

Section One - Production Stages

The process to make a video is relatively simple and logical. We need to think about what we're going to produce, organise it, produce/create it and then share it. This means that productions breaks down into the following four stages:

1. Preproduction
2. Production
3. Postproduction
4. Delivery

Preproduction

This is where we do all the work to understand what the right thing to create is. This pre-creative/brief-writing stage is arguably the most important in the whole process. This is often not given enough time in the desire to get on with the hands-on project. Needless to say, clear insight gained here is far cheaper to put into action than that gained when the film is finished and delivered. It's remarkable how many times I've made films with global brands, only to reach the end of the process and have someone who wasn't consulted early enough ask, "Why are we making this, anyway?"

Once we have this, we can start to think about how you're going to achieve all those objectives. This is known as creative or scripting. Creative tends to go through a number of iterations, until everyone is happy with it. I go into a lot more detail on this section in Chapter 9.

Once we have an agreed creative idea, we can start to organise all the things that are required to accomplish it. This will include an outline of the different actors/interviewees, props and locations. Making a film is very similar to organising an event. The event of physically making the film is called production.

Production

The hands-on production of the film is usually relatively short compared to the rest of the project. It's also often the most expensive stage in the project. This is because we can have lots of people in the same place at the same time. As we covered earlier in the book, the cost of the production phase has come down drastically since the days of scores of crew being required to get a decent-looking result. Today, a single self-shooting director/filmmaker can achieve a surprisingly high-quality output. That said, there are still elements that can add to the cost of the project. These include having a large number of actors/extras, shooting in locations that require travel/accommodation for the team, and specialist production elements such as drones, underwater cameras and cranes.

Postproduction

Once it's all been shot – 'in the can', if you like – the film then goes into the edit. An editor goes through all the material that was gathered during the production phase and selects the best moments from what could amount to hours of material. Many purists argue that this is true filmmaking, as it's where the film is actually made.

The first step is to get to an initial assembly cut. This is made up of all the best shots, which are pulled into a basic running order. This is also called a rough cut. The film now goes through a series of back-and-forths between the editor/producer and the various project stakeholders. If the editor is 'chunking' (splitting) the video for a number of different edits to be shared on social channels, he/she will tend to work on one main output and get that right before moving on to the other cuts. This allows the editor to familiarise himself/herself with the footage and to establish a style that the stakeholders are happy with.

Three Films?

It's said that, in the process of making a film, the creators actually produce three: there is the film that was initially conceived in the creative phase, the film that they believed they shot during production and then the film that is actually there once the editor has finished his/her work. Needless to say, it's the third film that remains to be shared and known by the world beyond the production team. This trope underlines an important aspect of filmmaking: be clear on what you're trying to achieve, but be prepared to incorporate positive additions as they occur. It's almost impossible to plan for every single eventuality that might befall the production. The best work comes from taking the events that occur – a beautiful sunset, a perfectly timed bird flying through the shot or an accidental nudge of an edit that just works – and being ready to integrate them.

Finishing

Once the project sponsor is happy with the edit, it's sent for a few final tweaks. At this stage, the titles, graphics and any final visual flourishes are added to the film. The picture is then considered to be 'locked'. This means that no one can make any more changes to the project's visuals.

Then, the edit is colour graded. This step tweaks and stylises the colours to make sure that they are all uniform and stylistically fit the story. For example, adding a blue hue to scenes filmed at night.

Sound design

The film is then sent to have the audio finished off. This includes having any sound effects and composed music added. Then, the sound designer tweaks all the levels of the audio to make sure that the volume is consistent, the dialogue is audible and it all sounds right. With modern content becoming as disposable as it has, this may not happen on every production. In that case, it comes down to the editor to give the film a once-over to make sure it's all good instead.

Delivery

We now have the finished output/outputs, but the whole process has been for nothing if the target audience don't get to see it/them. This is where the delivery method comes in. There are many, many different ways of getting your content seen, from Facebook banners to bus-mounted video screens. What is really worth doing, though, is including the distribution method in the briefing phase. This allows the production to be tailored to make the most of the displays that the outputs will be shown on or the different ways that people view each platform. I'll come to creating a really effective distribution plan a little later, in Chapter 14.

Section Two - Production Roles

There are a number of different roles involved in the production process. I've included this brief list so that you can keep up with whom is responsible for what. Each production company may work in a slightly different way, but the responsibilities are more or less the same. Nearly all of these functions are required on every production – even if they are all performed by the same person. Larger budgets allow for more time, and more time allows for more people.

Preproduction

Creative/scriptwriter

The creative comes up with the main idea (or ideas) and then creates the initial proposal document, which will help you understand exactly what you're getting. This may include the mood board (a collection of images that give an idea of what the project will look like), the storyboard (a shot by shot – usually drawn – illustration of the structure of the video) and any additional references that might be necessary.

He/she also writes and refines the script.

Producer

The producer is the organiser. He/she is responsible for bringing together all of the elements required for the production. He/she is the lynchpin, in that they are responsible for making sure that the film is delivered on brief, on budget and on time. As part of this, he/she will pull together the project costing and schedule, which will be added into the initial proposal document at the outset of the project. He/she will also be responsible for all the bookings for the project, from crew, equipment and onscreen talent to travel. He/she is usually the main point of contact for the client throughout the process.

Production

Director

The director is responsible for the artistic vision of the project. He/she works with the script and the producer to plan the execution of the shoot. On set, he/she will have a clear idea of what he/she wants the finished film to look like, and will coral the rest of the team to achieve this. The days of the 'auteur' film director – one who will happily trample over anyone to achieve, with a distinctive, unshakeable vision – are happily behind us. Most good directors now – in particular, those in the fast-moving world of brand films – are able to think on their feet, lead a team and use an in-depth understanding of their craft to adapt to the world around them.

Director of Photography (DoP)/cinematographer

The DoP is responsible for the camera/camera team and the way each shot looks. This means that he/she will often operate the camera (shoot the film) and do the lighting on set. Usually, having a separate DoP is reserved for larger productions.

Self-shooting director

As technology has become easier to use and budgets have shrunk, it has become more common for a director to play the role of the DoP at the same time. This leads to him/her being referred to as a self-shooting director.

Camera assistant/focus puller

The camera assistant is responsible for looking after the camera and lenses. He/she is also responsible for marking distances and keeping the shot in focus. (Only used on larger productions.)

Sound recordist

Erm, they record the sound. They can make all the difference to a production that has been shot in a noisy location. He/she is most likely to say, "Can someone turn that air conditioning off?", and is least likely to say, "Don't worry, we can get rid of that police siren in post."

First assistant director (AD)

The first assistant director (1st AD) is responsible for helping the director to achieve his/her vision. He/she is the one who keeps the production running to time and makes sure that everything is in the right place at the right time. When used, he/she is the director's mouthpiece on set. (Only used on larger productions.)

Gaffer

He/she is responsible for setting and moving all of the lighting. (Only used on larger productions.)

Grip

He/she is responsible for mounting and positioning the camera. (Only used on larger productions.)

Spark

The electrician. Lots of production lighting requires huge amounts of power. To keep things working/safe, it's necessary to have a professional spark.

Postproduction

Editor

The editor is responsible for 'finding the film'. He/she watches all of the shots, and then selects the ones that he/she feels best tell the story that was outlined and agreed on in the preproduction stage. He/she will also have a significant hand in the impact of the finished film. It's amazing how important the editor is to the quality of the final film. Often, a poorly edited film can terrify on first viewing, only to be completely turned around once someone who knows what they are doing has taken the reins.

Preditor

A producer who edits their own films. Popular in magazine/news type content production.

Animator/motion graphic artist

Animators bring 2D illustrations, 3D models and inanimate objects to life. He/she is skilled at imbuing inanimate objects with the movement required to generate emotional connections with the audience. He/she may also be responsible for creating the design and storyboards for the animations.

Dubbing mixer/sound engineer

The dubbing mixer/soundie sorts out all of the audio levels in the final video, and adds any sound effects and audio flourishes. These play the important role of tying the audio and video together. The sound engineer will also make sure that the music that has been chosen fits to the edit/animation perfectly.

Colourist/colour grader

The colourist is responsible for the look of the finished film. Sometimes different shots might look different because of different lighting/colouring during the production – he/she can iron this out. He/she may also stylise the film, which is changing the way the video looks by increasing the contrast between colours or changing the colour saturation (a bit like adding filters on Instagram). While colourists used to work only on larger productions, consumer-accessible grading programs are making this step integral to nearly every production.

In Summary: The Video-Production Process

It's useful for you to understand the different stages of the production process. This is just an overview, but it should better equip you to understand quotations and production conversations.

The process breaks down into four stages:

1. Preproduction

Agreeing on the goals of the project, generating a brief, finding the right creative idea and then all the planning. This is the foundation of the whole process – get it right here and you lay the groundwork for a successful project.

2. Production

This is where the project gets made. This includes the live action or animation shoot (if necessary), audio recording, and the generation of any elements that will be useful for the postproduction phase.

3.   Postproduction

Postproduction includes editing, animating, sound designing and adding music. This stage sees what many people argue is the actual filmmaking, because this is where the carving of the finished, polished film emerges from the rock, so to speak. This is also where the film is given all the final tweaks, such as the addition of titles, audio mastering and colour grading.

4.   Delivery

Delivery is where we get the film in front of the people we want to see it. This can include repurposing it by cutting it into different lengths and sharing it on different platforms. Stages 1, 2 and 3 are considered to be the traditional filmmaking stages. I've included delivery as stage 4 because getting the output(s) seen is essential.

Production roles in brief:

Preproduction

Creative/scriptwriter – comes up with the idea, writes script.

Producer – responsible for making the production happen.

Production

Director – has/delivers the vision for the film

Director of Photography (DoP)/cinematographer – responsible for the look of the film

Self-shooting director – a camera operating director

Camera assistant/focus puller – looks after/focuses the camera

Sound recordist – records sound

First assistant director (1st AD) – helps organize things on set for the director

Gaffer – responsible for delivery of lighting plan

Spark – on-set electrician

Postproduction

Editor – crafts the film from the elements provided by production

Preditor – editing producer

Animator/motion graphic artist –   magics movement from stationary/ inanimate elements

Dubbing mixer/sound engineer – makes the output sound great and consistent

Colourist/colour grader – makes the output look great and consistent

In the next chapter, we're going to look at the stage where success in the whole process begins: writing a really clear brief.

CHAPTER 6

WRITING A WINNING BRIEF

In this chapter, we'll look at how to start your production on the right foot, with the most important element in the entire process: the brief. This is the cornerstone to every single successful project. This matters to you because, whether you're commissioning a branded feature film or a coffee morning, knowing what you're trying to achieve and within what stipulations is essential.

What Are You Trying to Achieve?

"Begin with the end in mind."[1]
– Steven Covey, *The Seven Habits of Highly Effective People*

The first question you need to answer before starting any project is this: what are you hoping to achieve? That is, what is the specific, measurable action that you're hoping to generate as a result of completing and sharing your project? If you start the process with a very clear idea of the desired end position, you stand a far better chance of actually achieving it. This may seem obvious, but I've worked on numerous projects where we get very close to the end of the process, and a senior client representative says, "Hang on a second, why are we doing this?"

You need to be completely clear on your reasoning. Clarity of focus and purpose is what defines effective corporate content. It's too easy to start before taking the time to agree among the stakeholders what the video/ video project will be used for. Resist the temptation here to seek consensus among stakeholders by including too many disparate goals. Many people will use the fact that you're creating a video to include other messaging. Bear in mind that everything included in the final output that doesn't specifically work to achieve the goal you set out will detract from its effectiveness. This may sound overly severe – of course films can be about more than one thing.

PUT RUBBISH IN, GET RUBBISH OUT

You need to stop your film's effectiveness from being watered down by including too many messages.

This is why the briefing stage is so important. It takes time, skill and discipline to agree on and write a really good, clear brief. This can be an extremely valuable experience, as it requires an alignment among the different stakeholders in the process. Having agreed on the content, you should write a brief that is clear and concise, but that is readable and engaging. You should try to bring what you're after to life, as the more effectively you can do this, the more likely you are to capture the imagination of someone who might know a potential subject. So many of the briefs that we receive as a company are dull, verbose and complicated. This makes sense, as they are very specific business documents, but they tend to elicit better responses if they are clear and have a little life to them.

The Briefing Document

CLIENT BRIEF				
Company Name		Website		
Contact Name		Details		
Project Title				
Date		Deadline		
Background	Motivations for the project. Market / competitive situation. Past experiences. Any other relevant information.			
Creative Brief				
	Main purpose	Entertain / Educate / Inspire / Convince / Instigate Change		
	Estimated length	<1 / 1–2 / 2–3 / 3–4 / 4–5 / >5 minutes		
	Key messages			
	Tone of voice	Professional / Humorous / Serious / Genuine, etc.		
	Positioning			
	Mandatory elements			
	Company purpose/values			
	Visual style	Corporate brand / Part of a campaign		
	What the audience will...	Think: Feel: Do:		
Communication Objectives	Why do you want to use film for this communication?			
Target Audience	Internal / External / Consumers / Business Demographics / Psychographics			
Film Type	Event / Workshop / Advert / Animation / Documentary / Drama / Edit / Interview			
What Video Formats Do You Need?				
Distribution / Where Will the Video Be Published?	Website / YouTube / Vimeo / LinkedIn / Twitter / Instagram / Internal			
Internal Approvals Process	Who will have the final sign-off on this project, and at what points will they be involved in feeding back / signing off the films?			
What Do You Need from Us?	Estimate / Quote / Creative Proposal / Pitch / Tender			
Budget Range (£k / $k)	<10 / 10–15 / 15–20 / 20–25 / 25–30 / 35–40 / 50+			
Useful Resources or Existing Assets				

Figure 7: A production brief

Once you have all of the goals for the project ironed out, you can fill in a briefing document. The briefing document is the bible for the project. It should include all the objectives for the production: the audience, desired action (what success looks like), budget, timeframe, delivery channels and key stakeholders. You should take the time to do one of these for every project you do, even if you're a little lighter on the information on the basic ones. The time taken to make sure that you've thought a bit about it will save you far more time, money and annoyance in the long run. Almost every project that doesn't end up as desired can be traced back to an incomplete or poorly thought out brief. It doesn't need to be super complicated, but it will help you make more-effective films.

> *"If I had only one hour to save the world, I would spend fifty-five minutes defining the problem, and only five minutes finding the solution."*

This quotation is often attributed to Albert Einstein. Whether or not he did ever say it, the central concept is key for us here. Time spent understanding the problem is time very well spent indeed. Writing a decent brief is a good way of doing this. If it's worth making a video about, it's worth writing a brief for.

Different producers will use slightly different documents. I've included the one we use at Casual on the previous page. While there will naturally be differences in layout, the information included will be the same. You can download the briefing document from: www.newfirebook.com/links

Writing the brief

Have a think about what you want from the project. What needs to be included? When do you want it by? What have you seen online/on TV that you think could provide a guide creatively? Get some of the project stakeholders together and discuss your thoughts. You want to get alignment at this stage, as it's a lot cheaper and easier to make changes now than when the crew have shot the video and delivered the edit.

As you fill in the brief, it's important to try to be disciplined about what you include. If you're worried about clarity or ambiguity, it might help to include examples. The clearer and more accurate you can be, the easier the production/creative team will find it to come up with something that will fulfil your requirements.

It might seem like there is a bit of crossover between some of the sections, but we've found that, by coming at the same topic from slightly different angles, we can reach a more thorough understanding of what our clients are after.

The facts

The first part of the briefing document includes the key facts that those working on the production need to know. These are self-explanatory and include which company it's for, who the project lead is going to be and the deadline.

Background

This section allows you, the commissioner, to put in as much relevant information as possible to help the production team to understand the backdrop to the production. This might include information on your company, any branding/marketing campaigns that the video might play a part of, and, potentially, information on what your competitors are doing. There is no wrong information here, per se. It just needs to be relevant and laid out as bullet points, so that it's easily intelligible to the team.

Creative brief

Main purpose

What is the film for? For example, are you recruiting technology-savvy graduates or trying to show older people how to use their new mobile phone?

Estimated length

How long do you need the film to be? This will naturally depend on where it's going to be shared (see Chapter 12.) Don't worry if you're not sure about this. The production/distribution team you're working with will be able to advise.

Key messages

What is the most important message you want the audience to take from the video? Generally, less is more; try to be really focused on one statement. Having more than one is possible, but that does risk diluting them in the audience's minds.

Tone of voice

What is the tone of the video? Serious, exciting or humorous? This should fit with the rest of the content produced in the associated marketing campaign. This generally aligns with your broader brand tone, but you do have the opportunity to push it a little.

Positioning

What do you want the audience to think of when they reflect on this piece of content, and, beyond that, you and your brand? Are you looking to be seen as visionary, informed, groundbreaking, energetic and brave? You want to decide what your niche is, and then try to win that space in the minds of the audience.*

Mandatory elements

Is there anything that has to make it into the project? Are there any company slogans, for example? Is there a new facility that you want to include? It may be an event that you want covered or even a jingle. Whatever it is, it's best to know at the outset, so it can be worked in.

Company purpose/values

Do you have a company purpose or set of values? Even if these are not explicitly included in the video, it helps for the production team to know them, so that they know when the values are mentioned and can draw them out if necessary.

---

*For further information on positioning, I recommend reading Positioning: The Battle for Your Mind by Al Ries and Jack Trout (see Further Reading for details).'

Visual style

What ideas do you have about what the output will look like? Do you have brand or campaign guidelines that you want it to adhere to? You may also choose to provide examples of films, or images that you'd like the production team to include in their thinking.

What the audience will think, feel and do

The most important aspect of any corporate production is the reaction that it will create in the audience. A useful way to consider this is by seeking to understand what you want the audience to think, feel and do as a result of seeing the project. As we've already seen, video is the most effective way to communicate emotion to an audience. Because of that, it's useful to know what that desired emotion is from the outset. If we can be clear on this and the thought process that we're aiming for, it gives a far better chance of driving the action – the thing that you want them to do.

Communication objectives

Is there any particular messaging the project needs to convey? How does it fit within your broader communications? What do you want the audience to know by the end of the video(s)? This depends on the type of output, of course; if it's a very emotive brand piece, there may be less material to convey, and for a learning-and-development film there may be quite a lot of information here. If you need to append additional information to the briefing sheet, that's fine. Of course, it does help to be as clear and simple as you can be, though.

Target audience

How much do you know about the target audience? This is covered in far more depth in the next chapter. Any information you can include here will help the team to come up with an approach that will deliver on your goals for the project.

Film type

What format do you expect the video to take? This may be an animation, a live broadcast or a promotional documentary. Whatever it is, detail it here.

Animated Interviewees

We were once briefed to interview a series of executives from a European energy company. The project sponsor said that she wanted the interviews to be animated. The producer asked if they wanted the animator on set and the client said that she did. Sure enough, the animator turned up and started drawing a few sketches of the interviewees.

Sabine, the client, asked what they were doing, and the producer explained. Sabine looked very bemused. "No, no. I meant animated!" she said, waving her arms around. "Aha!" The coin dropped to much laughter from all present. It turned out that they had received some very dry interviews in the past, and she just wanted to make sure that the executives came across as being as lively and interesting as possible.

The moral of the story, particularly when working with people who are operating in a second language, is to discuss in depth what is meant by the different elements of the brief, so that everyone understands them.

What video formats do you need?

There are a wide range of possible formats available. HD resolution is standard for all productions. You may need it at a higher resolution than that – 4K or even 8K. You might also choose to have it shot on an iPhone or delivered on DVD.

Distribution/where will the video be published?

How are people going to get to see the output? It's best to think about this now, as you want the production to be optimised for the format or platform – even if it's just your own company's intranet. (See Chapter 14.)

What do you need from us?

What are you expecting in response to this document? Most productions start with three creative treatments, each with a budget and timeframe. You may decide that you want the team to present the ideas to your team or create a short video to pitch it to your own stakeholders. Again, it's useful to know this, so that everyone in the process knows what to expect.

Internal approvals process

Who needs to see the production to sign it off? Does the main contact have the ultimate power to sign it off, or are there other sponsors who will need to see it to OK it? It might be necessary to get the video to the point where the first contact is happy with it, before showing the senior contact. This can increase the time and cost of the project. Whatever happens, it makes the process a lot smoother to have one person who is able to collate feedback and then deliver it in one go.

Budget range

What budget do you have available for the production? It can feel like you'll get a better deal if you hold this information back, and if you're not sure, of course you can do that. The budget is another of the constraints that the production team needs to work with. The process is extremely malleable, so you can make a film for the same brief for all different budget levels. What changes is the amount of time the team is able to spend developing an idea and then finessing the delivery. (See Chapter 8.)

Useful resources or existing assets

There is so much content being produced at the minute that the chances are that you'll have some material that can be included. This could be B-roll (supplementary footage used to cut away from the main subject of the film), past videos/commercials or music. Whatever it is, let the producers know, so that they can incorporate it if it fits.

Managing Multiple Stakeholders in the Creative Process

Once you have the central idea for the film, it's important that you don't allow it to be diluted/spoilt. You'll find that everyone involved in the process wants to have some input into the final piece. This is a perfectly natural desire; after all, what's the point in being involved in a process if you don't OK a part. As a very established director friend of mine says (a little disgustingly), "Everyone wants to do a tiny bit of pee on it before they sign it off." The danger of this is that it can lead to the video evolving away from the clear, central idea it had when it was first conceived.

As a filmmaker, I used to find this tendency quite challenging. When I first started down the path of making corporate films, I put my heart and soul into the work that I did. This led to challenges when the people paying wanted to make changes that I felt compromised the impact of the final output. What I learned was the importance of identifying the central concept for the video and then safeguarding that at all costs. Everything else can be tweaked or amended. The central idea is the one thing that you can't really change, because it's the foundation for everything else that you do. If you change this, you're making a different film.

Pick a point person for your project

It's important to remember that what goes in the brief ends up in the film. We were producing a series of films for a global cosmetics company. The department we were working with created a brief that they were happy with. They then sent it to the US business, who looked at it and said that it had to include some key elements that they had been working on. The same thing happened when it was shared with the Asia Pacific and South American marketing departments. These additional elements were added on rather than being worked into the initial concept.

The production team tried to explain that this would lead to the film taking on a slightly Frankenstein quality, but the client had lost control of the process internally; the other teams had become involved in the process and so they stayed involved – adding feedback and elements all the way through the project. The problem with this was that the film became confused and no longer achieved the initial concrete goal.

One way to overcome this is to always have a single leader for the project. Films become lightning rods for opinion, and highlight differences of opinion in an organisation. The production goes ahead to solve the challenge that the initial sponsor had. One way to avoid 'too many cooks' becoming involved is to understand what the new stakeholders are feeding back on. Is it the brand? Is it the way the project delivers against the initial brief? Or is it something else?

No matter what you're trying to deliver, there should be someone who is given the power to make the final call on the project. He/she is usually the person responsible for solving the challenge in the brief. This ties into the point on clarity – too many voices competing with one another risk creating a muddled message and unnecessary, costly reworkings. Choose a point person, and invest in them to deliver what is required. The results are always better.

TRY TO BE A LITTLE MORE FOCUSED IN DECIDING WHAT YOU'RE AFTER THAN THIS

Writing a Voiceover Script

Once you're happy with your idea, you can start to write a script. There are a few rules of thumb to work with here:

» Don't write anything that you can show in the picture.

» People read aloud at three words per second, so a minute of unbroken voiceover is 180 words.

» Allow about 10% of the time for the video to breathe, transition, etc. Because of this, we tend to keep a minute of video to about 165 words at most.

» Keep sentences short and punchy. They should each be 10 to 12 words maximum.

» Keep sentences simple. Avoid using sub-clauses wherever possible.

» Try to keep the language in the active rather than the passive voice, as this is more dynamic. This means the subject of each sentence performs the action. For example, saying, "The dressing drowned the cucumber," rather than saying, "The cucumber was drowned by the dressing"; or saying, "We offer great packages," rather than saying, "The packages we offer are great". This gives your sentences more energy.

In Summary: Writing a Winning Brief

It's important that you're clear on what you're trying to achieve from the outset. To do this, it's essential to fill in a briefing document. Having all of the stipulations agreed in black and white irons out differences at a stage when it's still really easy to deal with them. The further through the project you get, the more expensive fixes tend to be.

The briefing document should play a couple of different roles. On the one hand, it should be a consolidation of all the relevant information that everyone working on the project needs to know. The clearer and more comprehensive the brief, the better the thinking that it inspires. On the other hand, it's an anchor point for the whole project. It allows the team to refer back to what they are trying to achieve. It keeps them on the right track to achieving it.

Once you've completed the brief, it helps to appoint a single person to be responsible for running the project on your company's behalf. As much as possible, he/she should consolidate feedback and communications with the producers. This will help to avoid the risk of too many cooks becoming involved and the messaging getting muddled.

In the next chapter, we look at the next most important step in the process – effectively defining your target audience.

CHAPTER 7

DEFINING YOUR TARGET AUDIENCE

Once you're clear on what you're trying to achieve with your project, you should clarify exactly whom you need to reach to make it happen. Being clear about whom your audience are exactly is essential for everything content related that you do. It will enable you to do the following:

» Focus your marketing, so that it you only reach the people you want to: those who are interested in your service, job role or product. This reduces wastage, and saves cost and time.

» Create content designed to engage a specific persona, which improves engagement and conversions.

» Develop long-term relationships with your audience by sharing content that is TRUE for them.

This knowledge will allow you to create content that is 'right' for the audience. As we covered at the beginning of this book, great content is now at everyone's fingertips. What will set you apart is having content that resonates perfectly with the people you're trying to influence. Relevance is essential. 'Broadcasting' in the literal sense – spreading a message to a wide audience – can now be 'narrowcasting' instead. This makes it far more cost-effective, as you're only reaching the people you really want to reach. To do this, though, you must be crystal clear on who they are.

As we discussed in Chapter 3, having a clear understanding of your audience, and their viewpoints, cultural references and interests will significantly increase the impact of your spend. This means that you need to think carefully about who the target audience of your stories are. With all of this research, you'll want to scale the amount you put into it to the size of the project/campaign that will result. You'll spend considerably more time and research, in far greater detail, for your main, strategic marketing campaign for the year than you will for a one-off newsletter for an event.

A common mistake that many people make is to try to produce work that is relevant to too broad an initial group. Remember that the more specific you are, the more chance you have of engaging the audience and landing your message effectively. You should aim for your content to be extremely valuable/ useful to your audience. It's easier to do this if you tailor it very specifically to a niche. Once you've cornered one audience grouping, you can look at growing the group outwards. Avoid being too general to start with.

Personalisation

This whole process is ultimately about personalisation – creating content for the specific people who make up your target group. As the tools develop for marketers to know their audience and to tailor content, it will become more and more specific to the individual (data-protection rules notwithstanding – see box on page 201). This represents an exciting development for content producers. Netflix, for example, say that it has 33 million different versions of its site.[1] Each one reflects the different personalities and watching habits of its customers.

Primary vs secondary audience

It's important to define and focus on your primary audience, as the majority of the content that you produce will be for them. On the other hand, bear in mind that there may well be secondary audiences for your content.

The *primary audience* are the people who you need to reach to achieve the objectives you've set. They are the people who'll take the specific action you require.

The *secondary audience*, on the other hand, are the people who will influence the members of the primary audience. These may be family members, friends, colleagues or social media influencers.

Once you've identified whom these people are, the process of understanding their profile and the type of content you should be producing for them is the same as for the primary audience.

Defining Your Target Audience

There are a few key elements to consider about your audience. These will help you to paint a clear image of them, and will make it easier to think about the kind of content that will work for them. What are they?

Demographics

Demographics cover a range of facts that illustrate who the audience member is. There are huge amounts of data available online, which is one of the main reasons that the major social networks and e-commerce sites have been able to make such vast amounts of money. Data is hugely valuable, and yet most web users are happy to give theirs away in return for the 'free' usage of the service. This huge amount of data means that these companies can charge large amounts for marketing, because the information they have means that marketing messages can be extremely targeted.

Examples of demographic information are listed as follows:

- Age
- Sex
- Income
- Occupation
- Education
- Marital status
- Religion
- Race
- Ethnicity
- Sexual orientation
- Generation

Geographics

Geographics are similar to demographics in that they are also facts. You can just spread your net to include a smaller or wider grouping of them. Do be aware that these may be impacted from visits by bots (see box on page 200). Geographics include the following:

- House
- Street
- Village
- Town
- City
- Region
- Nation
- Continent
- Hemisphere
- Global

An example

The major issue is that information is just data. It doesn't tell you enough about the underlying motivations of the target persona. This can lead to challenges. For example, we may be looking to target this person:

» Male
» Over 60 years old
» High net worth
» Divorced
» Has children
» Drives expensive cars
» Lives in a large house
» Has pets

The Prince of Wales   *The Prince of Darkness*

This unlikely pairing both fall into the aforementioned data pool.* Because of this, it's useful to consider other factors that are more instructive of the type of content they may engage with.

Psychographics

psychographics

sʌɪkə(ʊ)ˈgrafɪks

plural noun

"The study and classification of people according to their attitudes, aspirations and other psychological criteria, especially in market research."[2]

Where demographics are a collection of objective data, psychographics are subjective information. This makes them extremely useful for marketers, because they allow us to understand the audience's motivations.

---

* *Thanks to Richard Purvis from Crunch Simply Digital for this example.*

Once we understand these, we can start to communicate with them in a way that will engage and drive them to action.

Psychographics are also known as IAO variables: *interests, activities* and *opinions.* I find it more helpful to think of them in this way, as it makes it easier to think about, and the word 'psychographics' sounds pretty much like jargon. IAO information is, by its nature, fuzzier than the solid, black-and-white facts of demographics. In reality, it's far more useful.

On top of interests, activities and opinions, psychographic information includes personality, values and lifestyle. These give us a far clearer way of thinking about what will engage the audience member, as we can see here:

Demographic view *Psychographic view*

Demographic view:

»   Male

»   Mid-thirties

»   Lives in Brooklyn, NY

»   Married

»   Born in the UK

Psychographic view:

»   Plays guitar in a band

»   Likes travel, festivals & gigs

»   Loves pie and chips

»   Subscribes to Rolling Stone

»   Follows Radiohead on Instagram

By looking at the previous information, we can see just how valuable the psychographic information is to someone looking to create content for this man. The demographic information could point us towards anyone from a banker working on Wall Street to a youth-group worker or a dustman – this makes targeting them challenging. You could take out a billboard in Manhattan, for example, but that's not exactly cost-effective/efficient.

The psychographic information, on the other hand, allows us to understand exactly how to communicate on a level that will engage him. For example, we could share trailers for a video series on a road trip to a festival in South Africa. We could enhance the offer with a competition to win tickets and travel to the same festival next year. We're only able to offer this because we understand what makes our target audience tick.

Once you know what the audience likes/wants/needs to watch, then you can look at what you do as a company, and see what you can create and share for them. There is naturally a fine balance to creating the content that people want to watch and plugging your company/products. As we examined in Chapter 4, the content that you produce should lie at the intersection between what will be of value to your identified audience and your purpose as a business.

Creating target-audience personas

A target-audience persona is a fictional person who exhibits the characteristics of your target audience.
This helps you to think more clearly about them.

This is where the whole audience-targeting process gets creative. Rather than thinking about target-audience groupings as an amorphous mass of people – which is where it's easy to go wrong (targeting millennials is an archetypal example of this*) – it helps to create a stereotyped individual.

---

*Although it's often put forwards as a target grouping, a millennial is anyone born between 1982 and 2000. This is far too broad a category to engage effectively, certainly with a single output. You need to be far more specific by adding in more criteria with which to differentiate them.

Or, better still – to reflect the wider group – five stereotyped individuals. Each character should be (as much as possible) a living, breathing character with a backstory. This will help you think about the different ways that you can engage them.

Start by giving them a memorable name, for example:

» Tracy the Techie

» Simon the Scientist

» Grace the Graduate

» Tim the Trainee

This helps to kickstart your creative thinking for the next stage.

Paint a picture of their character by asking questions about them and the things they do. This is best done with a few members of the team, so you can bounce suggestions off each other.

Questions might include the following:

» Where do they live?

» Where do they get their news?

» What do they do at the weekend?

» What music do they listen to?

» What blogs do they read?

» What are their hopes/dreams/goals?

» What's the first thing they think about in the morning?

Pain points

One of the most important things to know about any audience is what their 'pain points' are. These are their concerns or fears: the things that keep them up at night. The main reason for their high value to us, as communicators, is that the fear of loss is a far greater motivator for action than the promise of gain. People obviously have a very wide range of these, from the minor (e.g. finding a parking space) to the existential fear of illness and death. As you can tell from this last – maybe crass – example, you want to be very careful how you use these. You want your content to assist, not fearmonger among your audience. You should know their fears, so that you can know how to remedy or soften them.

Pain-point questions might include these:

» What keeps them up at night?

» What are they worried about at work?

» What is the hardest thing they have to deal with day to day?

» What is their greatest fear/insecurity?

» What annoys them about something that they do regularly?

For example, a new parent might be very interested in content that helps them live the life they led before they had their baby.

Gathering data

Once you have a clear idea of the questions that you want to answer, you should fill in as many of them as possible that you know. You may already have much of the information you need. Try to build up as much of a picture of the different personas as possible. There are a few different ways that you can gather the data you need to do this:

✓ Share a survey with existing customers

✓ Interview clients

✓ Use social media tracking/monitoring tools; e.g. Facebook Dashboard

✓ Research websites/forums/blogs

✓ Evaluate your website/use Google Analytics

✓ Look at Quora/Reddit

Bear in mind that some of the online data may be generated by bots. Because of this, you need to make a sharp assessment as to how much you can trust.

Be thorough and discount information that is false. If you're unsure, look at ways that you know are secure – interviews, blogs from known sources, and focus groups.

Data Gathering with Premium Content

One way of gathering data on your audience is by offering premium content on your owned channels. This is content where the value to the audience is enough for them to be happy to enter their details to access/watch it. Many websites do this with e-books and webinars. There is no reason why you can't do this with video content. To do this, you have to have established the value for the viewer. The amount of information you can gather is diverse, from emails (which will help you with retargeting later) through to interests, and even how much they are prepared to spend in your market in the next year. The more the perceived value to the audience, the more information they are willing to share to access it.

Sharing content for your target group

Once you have clear personas agreed, you can start to think about the type of content that they will respond to. This should feed into the briefing document that we covered earlier..

You should also think about where that content should be distributed to get the best engagement from your target group.

> One of the great things about sharing content online is that it allows you to target your audience with remarkable accuracy.

It also allows you to see how the audience grouping responds to different types of content, which, in turn, allows you to tailor the message/content to get the best response. This could be as simple as changing the title or thumbnail image, right through to full reshoots/re-edits. This is covered in much more depth in Chapter 14.

Being a Customer-centred Content Company

One of the most useful things to consider when thinking about your audience is where in the buying-and-consideration process they are. This is known as the 'buyer journey'. This is important because it significantly changes their viewpoint, and thus the type of content you should use to engage them. In the past, this was known as the 'buying funnel'. Suspects/prospects would be fed in at the top, and, through a process of building trust, they would flow down to the point where they would make the purchase and become a customer.

The customer lifecycle loop

Autodesk's director of content marketing and social media, Dusty DiMercurio, explained in his presentation at ThinkContent in New York in 2018, that this model isn't really reflective of reality.[3] According to him, Autodesk's content made a significant positive shift when it started to think in terms of the ongoing cycle. He feels that the traditional funnel approach puts too much weight on the sale stage. The goal is to support your customers/buyer with their new purchase, continuing to build affinity and brand value, so that they recommend you and buy again. This is particularly important for a software-as-a-service (SaaS) company, which effectively needs to remake the sale every month. This is illustrated below:

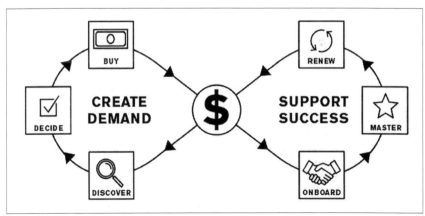

Figure 8. The customer lifecycle loop

As you can see from the different stages in the diagram, you need to create different types of content depending on where in the process your audience are. The phases break down as follows.

Discover

This is the top of the traditional funnel. At this stage, you want to share content that highlights problems that you can solve and possibly problems that you're working on solutions for. This is where the hero content discussed in Chapter 3 would fit.

Decide

Here, you want to help people who are researching your products. By now, they probably have a shortlist of companies that they are reviewing. To influence them, clearly illustrate the solutions, benefits and value propositions that your products offer. This content needs to cover all of the possible concerns that potential nay-sayers in the process might have. Case studies and testimonials work really well here.

Buy

This content should assist the purchase and support the customer to get the maximum value from their investment.

Onboard

This content should support your customers in understanding and getting the most out of their new product.

Master

This stage builds on the content shared in the onboarding phase, but builds on it to give your customers an even more in-depth understanding of the product.

Renew

This phase shares new benefits with the customer. It reminds them that you haven't forgotten about them and that you care about their concerns.

Roles your content must play

Ideally, all of the content that you produce should be designed to help your audience at a stage in this cycle. If you zoom out from the individual stages, it's possible to look at the content as fulfilling three roles:

1. **Creating demand**

   On the left side of the diagram, this content aims to attract the audience and convert them into customers.

2. **Supporting success**

   On the right side of the diagram, this content helps customers to fully access and appreciate the value of your services.

3. **Building brand affinity**

   As we covered in Chapter 3, all of the content that you create should personify your brand and build affinity with it among your audience. This will allow you to gain attention and influence in your market.

You can see the breakdown of these three areas below:

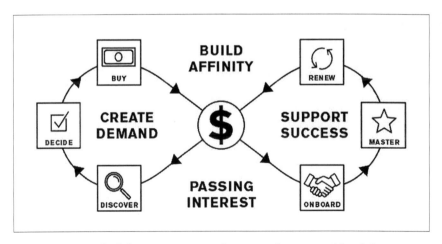

Figure 9. The different requirements of content in the customer lifecycle loop

Audience Targeting in B2B Marketing

One of the challenges of B2B selling is that there is nearly always more than one person responsible for the buying decision. It is, of course, true that each member of the buying team – or decision-making unit (DMU) – is a human with very human motives within the process. That said, the different members of the group have different motivations. Understanding these can help you to target them with messaging that will help them in their decision-making process.

The different roles played are as follows. One person might play more than one role. The different members of the DMU need slightly different types of content to keep the process moving.

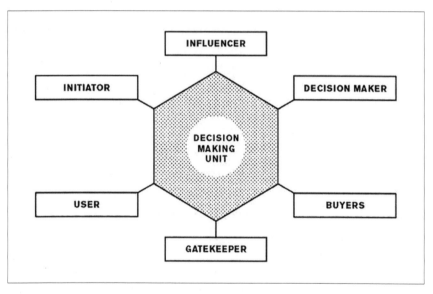

Figure 10. The key to understanding the B2B buying process: the decision-making unit

By understanding the role that each plays, you can make sure that they see what you need them to:

1. Users have a problem that can be solved by your product. They are

the ones who will actually use it and are key to the evaluation of the product/service. The content that will appeal to them illustrates a thorough understanding of the product. It will demonstrate improved usability/efficiency/ease of use. This content may also be emotive, as you're trying to make them drive the action of procurement.

2. Users often take the role of initiators, because they know the tool and so recognise a need to solve a certain problem. They then start looking for a way to solve it. They are generally the buying-process sponsor and are the most important person in the unit. Content, for them, is similar to that for the users, but it also needs to support them through the process.

3. Influencers have a standing within the unit that allows them to outline the stipulations the product must conform to, or to exert pressure over which supplier/product is chosen. Influencer marketing has blossomed and is covered in more depth in Chapter 2.

4. Buyers are responsible for physically buying the product. They generally work in the procurement function of the business and tend to have a checklist – physical or otherwise – of objective requirements for the solution to deliver against. Content for them should focus on tangible benefits: cost savings or time efficiencies for the business, for example.

5. Gatekeepers are the individuals who control the flow of the buying process. They may shield the senior members of the process from unwanted contact.

6. Decision makers are usually senior members of staff. They will consider the information gathered by the initiators, gatekeepers and buyers, and make the final decision. They need to see content that helps them to evaluate the purchase, so clear information on the features and benefits of the product is useful here.

In Summary: Defining Your Target Audience

Creating great content that resonates with and works for your target audience, starts with knowing who they are. This is the first step towards personalising your content. There are a few different types of information you need to understand to correctly categorise your audience.

There are two main types of information – demographic and psychographic. Demographics are facts about the audience, including where they live, what they earn, the job they have, etc. Psychographics are more useful because they tell us about the thought processes of the audience. They are things that the audience are interested in. This helps us to understand how to communicate with the audience.

Creating audience personas

Once you've gathered some information on your audience groups, you can start to create personas of stereotyped members of the group. This will help you to more accurately tailor the content to them. Start by giving them names that help to kick start the thinking process; for example, Tracy the Techie.

Then, go through the process of filling out the type of person they are by answering a wide range of questions about them. There are a number of online tools that will help you do this. One of the more valuable exercises is to think about the pain points they might have. These might vary from the significant – a fear of death – to the mundane – missing the bus each morning. They help us to understand why people act in the way that they do. Understanding this will allow you to create content that inspires them to take certain actions.

The customer journey

Understanding where your audience members are in the buying funnel/ process helps to create content that they will find useful. The type of video that someone who has just bought your product is interested in is different from what they will want to see if they are casually perusing the market, for example.

In the next chapter, we're going to look at some of the things to think about when setting the budget for your project.

CHAPTER 8

SETTING THE BUDGET

The next thing to consider is how much budget you want to put to work in accomplishing your objectives. On the one hand, the process of filmmaking is creative, so the budget becomes an additional constraint that the creative thinking needs to work around. Because of this, it can be extremely flexible – it's possible to fulfil the same objectives for significantly different investment levels. On the other hand, quality, in-depth thinking and delivery take time, and time costs money.

More Money Doesn't Always Make For better Filmmaking

There, I said it.

When I first started making films professionally, I always wanted to work with bigger crews and more equipment – toys – such as helicopters, cranes and camera cars. All these gismos and the people to operate them are part of what made film production pre-2005 extremely expensive and time consuming. What I've learned since then is that smaller is often better. Two- or three-person crews are able to think on their feet and react to events as they happen around them. This makes them more flexible, and, ultimately, allows them to be more creative if time is limited.

That isn't to say that more budget doesn't get you more, but it's far better to make sure that any additional investment goes on time – that is, thinking, working, shooting, editing and animating time. That way, you're able to get to tangibly better productions in return for your additional investment. Resist the temptation to go big, with all the ego, excitement and razzmatazz that a large crew brings – not to mention the catering van. They burn cash in a way that isn't necessarily visible 'on the screen'; i.e. to your audience.

Having said that, the cost of getting aerial, Steadicam or minicam shots has gone through the floor, so not splurging on expensive equipment doesn't necessarily mean less dynamism for your film.

It's about where you put it...

For years, there has been a disconnect between where marketing money gets spent and where the real potential lies. In studies, researchers have found that the quality of creative messaging is responsible for up to 75% of a campaign's success.[1;2] In spite of this, as much as 90% of the overall spend is often still focused on the media budget.

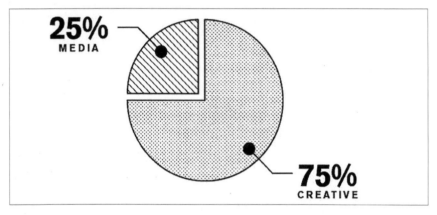

Figure 11. Factors contributing to the effectiveness of your campaign

The Power of Creative Messaging

This is a Casual Films case study, but bear with me... Charity Breast Cancer Now wanted to create a series of films to help it to stand out. The market for cancer charities in the UK is extremely crowded.

It's the charity's aim to eliminate cancer by the year 2050 through researching cures. The idea behind the campaign was to position *everyone* involved in the charity as playing a role in curing cancer. The campaign's aim was to encourage donations. The creative suggested that anyone making a donation was curing cancer too. This insight was based on the famous conversation that John F. Kennedy (JFK) had with a janitor while visiting NASA. JFK asked the man what he was doing, and the janitor replied, "I'm putting man on the moon, sir."

The videos were edited from five profiles with people involved in the charities. In total, there were nearly 50 separate outputs, including a 90-second cut of each profile and a number of shorter cuts for social media. The videos featured people affected by cancer – family members, cancer survivors and terminal sufferers. This made for a powerful combination. The shorter-form social cuts were able to trail the contents of the main videos. Their contents provided a very effective hook. So effective that they achieved the following results.

Around 16% of the way through the campaign budget, the videos had beaten the view target for the whole campaign by 2,251% (115,670 full length views). The average session duration on the Breast Cancer Now website increased by 145%. Across all platforms, it had delivered 1.5 million impressions with 462,000 engagements.

> The campaign is one of the most successful we've ever done.

But why does this matter? Because the campaign was extremely successful. The main reason for this wasn't the media spend, or even the quality of the filmmaking; it was the quality of the stories. The central idea – donators are curing cancer – is a good one, but it was the powerful emotional content that engaged the audience and drove the result. Of course, most business communicators don't have such compelling content to work with. Whatever the subject of your project, though, make sure you spend the time to find the best possible people to feature. This is time well spent when it comes to maximising its effectiveness.

The ability to demonstrate efficacy is key. Traditional TV-commercial-driven marketing became so successful largely because of how strong the metrics that were available to support it were. One of the major challenges that online content has faced over the years is the challenge of showing direct causation between money spent and the return on that investment.

But this isn't necessarily about spending more money on marketing than you already are. Creating and executing a comprehensive and effective content strategy can be about redistributing the money you're already investing. Why, for example, are you spending hundreds of thousands or even millions of dollars on the production of TV commercials when the vast majority of your audience watch them for the first time as a small image on their Facebook feed, momentarily pausing before scrolling onwards, and paying very little attention to them. Ad blockers and on-demand TV viewing make it challenging to even get through to the audience.

For years, marketers have been chasing the mirage of the 'viral' video (see Chapter 14). Examples such as the fantastically successful Dollar Shave Club commercial create the impression that, with just the right output, businesses can share a cheap video and it will be shared globally without any paid push. This is, alas, a fallacy and has been damaging to the perception of what is required to make a video succeed online.

In reality, you need a strong, audience-appropriate message that is packaged in a creative, well-produced video, and marketed in just the right way to gain traction.

This kind of focus and specialisation requires budget. You need enough money to make the videos at an appropriate quality, and then enough to amplify them and get them seen by the target audience. The money that you put against this should align with how important these goals are for the broader organisation.

More budget will generally lead to better results. It costs money to get people who know what they're doing to wrap your message in a compelling story and then translate it to the screen effectively, for it to be seen by the people you want.

Dollar Shave Club

One of the most famous and successful online promos of recent years was the "Our Blades are F***ing Great" spot produced by Dollar Shave Club. The video features the founder/CEO walking through the company warehouse delivering an informative and hilarious piece to camera. Launched in March 2012, the video inspired over 12,000 orders on that first day alone and drove the successful launch of the company. Dollar Shave Club was acquired by Unilever for $1 billion just four years later.

This is a brilliant example of the power of video in the Internet age. It was viral in the true sense of the world, and, at the time of writing, it has nearly 26 million views. It's budget of $4,500 is often touted as a reason for businesses to be extremely cost conscious in the video they produce. It's not quite as simple as this, though. Michael Dubin, the founder/CEO and star of the video had spent years working in the marketing industry, and even had some acting experience. It's estimated that to create a similar film, without this background or these skills, a company would need to spend around $40K. This is still a comparatively small amount next to the revenue and valuation it was able to drive.

From the outset, Dubin used his branding experience to make all of Dollar Shave Club's products and marketing the perfect match for it's target market. The 'Blades' video and the variety of other similarly toned content that it has shared over the years, sets the tone for a brand that people want to be a part of.

Things That Affect Budget

As we've previously covered, the production process can be flexed to accommodate every level of budget for almost every brief. You've probably seen the following diagram before; if not, you're probably familiar with the concept. In essence cost, time and quality are interlinked. When you pull one stipulation in, it pushes out the others, so you can only choose two of them. So, if you want something to be made quickly, the cost increases, unless you're happy for the quality of production to reduce.

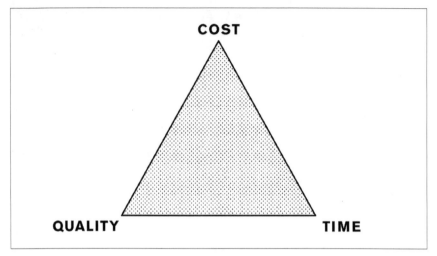

Figure 12. The time/cost/quality triangle

What else affects budget?

There are a number of questions that you might want to consider that will impact the cost of the production. This is in no way an exhaustive list; it's only meant as a guideline on the breadth of possible elements:

- » Who is going to make it? Internal/external/freelancers?
- » Where are you going to get your project in front of your audience?
- » What role does video play in your wider marketing/communications make-up?
- » What resources do you already have that could be repurposed?
- » Are there other 'pots' of budget that you could borrow from if the project were able to hit additional touchpoints?
- » At what stage of the process are major changes made?

» Do you want to create a number of re-edits; for social media, for example?

» Do you want to feature a particular talent on screen or for the voiceover/music? You can always use your own people or library music to reduce the cost.

» Might it be helpful to pay for the initial creative to help you sell via a particular route?

» Think about economies of scale. How could you shoot with future projects in mind? Could you create a template film?

» Do you have to shoot interviews, or could you just use audio interviews?

» Would one piece of hero content work, or would multiple smaller films work better?

» How future proof do you need it to be? Do you want to include that in the creative thinking about the production?

» What references do you want to share with the creative team? Even if it's a big-budget production, there might be a cheaper way of doing the same thing.

In Summary: Setting the Budget

How much you put aside for your production is naturally up to you. It depends on how important the objectives are to your business. Film is an extremely flexible medium, so, in most cases, it's possible for the creative team to flex the idea and production around what you have available. You do, of course, get what you pay for, though. If you need a video to welcome people to your website, giving a camera to an intern and expecting them to create something that befits such an important role lies somewhere between wishful thinking and negligence.

Where possible, you should try to focus any additional budget on time, rather than larger crews, lenses or equipment, as this is more likely to show in the impact of the final output. I don't mean you should never use these things – there are times when they will reap the best possible rewards for you – but it's more that you want to think about how each line item in the quotation will impact the people who consume the content.

Finally, if you need a specific grouping of people to see the film, be prepared to invest in getting it in front of them. There is more information on this in Chapter 14 on distribution. Push-free 'viral' marketing doesn't exist.

CHAPTER 9

GETTING THE RIGHT CREATIVE IDEA

There are thousands of filmmakers out there who could make you a stunning-looking film. What sets the great ones apart is the quality of their creative thinking, and how well that answers and enlivens the confines of the brief. The quality of the creative idea is the most significant differentiating factor between good and bad work. A great idea can be produced on a shoestring and the idea will still shine through. No amount of Hollywood razzmatazz can save a terrible idea, which you can witness every weekend at your local cinema.

The Case for Creativity

"Creatively awarded campaigns deliver 11x the return on investment of non-creatively awarded campaigns."

– James Hurman, *The Case for Creativity*[1]

According to a number of different research studies, up to 75% of a campaign's effectiveness is defined by the quality of the creative messaging.[2;3] This means that getting this bit right is essential for maximising your return on investment and succeeding with your content strategy.

In this chapter, we'll spend some time looking at how to come up with ideas that will make your content stand apart.

"Inspiration exists, but it must find you working."

– Pablo Picasso

Ideas for great work can come from anywhere. It really helps to have an open mind with respect to different sources of inspiration that you might come across in your day-to-day life. I've always found that the best way to come up with ideas is to go through the brief in depth, so that you're fully 'inside' what you're trying to achieve, the audience and possible techniques. I then find it useful to spend a couple of days mulling it over before settling on something.

This reflects James Webb Young's method outlined in his 1940s book, *A Technique for Producing Ideas*. It might be 80 years old, but it works as well as ever.[4]

A technique for producing ideas

Step 1: Gather

Get as much background information as you can. Try to understand exactly what the problem is (this is where a really good/thorough brief comes in handy – see Chapter 6). Look for inspiration from the ways that people have communicated on this issue before. Have a look at your inspiration scrapbook (see box on opposite page). You want to fully immerse yourself in the brief.

Step 2: Think

Start playing with different ideas. Ask lots of questions; for example, can we combine x with y? Try juxtaposing different ideas on top of each other. Keep going until you can't do it anymore.

Step 3: Forget

Move on to other things, but keep the problem in mind. Go for a walk, listen to a podcast, visit a museum or gallery, or just continue with your work. Mull the idea over in the background.

Step 4: Idea!

If you've worked through the first three steps properly, you'll find that an idea should just pop into your head. This may well happen when you least expect it – you might find it useful to keep a pencil and paper beside your bed, so that you can write down any late-night inspiration and go back to sleep without worrying about forgetting it.

Step 5: Craft

Finally, you'll need to hone your idea into something that answers all facets of the brief. This requires work to make it just right. You should make sure it works visually and conceptually. Like any diamond pulled from the rough, you'll need to spend time polishing it to make it really sparkle.

Keeping an Inspiration Scrapbook

We're all subjected to so much content that it can be difficult to keep track of all the different inspirations that you might choose to draw on. Because of this, it's useful to keep a scrapbook of different ideas that you've seen, which you think might work one day. This could be as simple as creating a playlist on YouTube or a pin board on Pinterest. You could also download imagery into a folder, ready to be included in a PowerPoint/Keynote presentation when you want to review it. However you decide to do it, it makes the process of reviewing ideas and techniques significantly less frustrating if you have everything you need already laid out.

Brainstorms

I've always had a bit of a love-hate relationship with creative brainstorms. It's useful to have everyone who is going to be involved in the process in the room to discuss the project. Where I think they fall down is when you open it to the wider company, and get too many people together who don't quite understand the brief. The ideas tend to be fairly superficial, and lack the creative depth to hit all the points on the brief. If they are used as a starting point, they can still play a role, particularly if the aim is to get all those involved in the process to feel like they have some agency in the idea.

For any size company, getting a large number of people together in a room is expensive. I've found that, while you never quite know where a good idea will come from, brainstorms do have a bit of a tendency to degenerate and stop delivering useful ideas relatively quickly – after about 40–45 minutes. To that end, here are a few tips on running a fruitful brainstorming session:

✓ Nominate as *chair*, someone who has had the time to really understand the brief.

✓ The chair starts the session by reading the brief, explaining any ambiguities and answering questions.

✓ He/she then shares any inspirations or additional material.

✓ The chair takes notes on a large page/flipchart/whiteboard, so that the group can see what has been discussed.

✓ Consider starting the session by getting people to discuss the brief in twos, or even work on it on their own, before reconvening as a group to discuss findings. This is a method that Hassan Rafiq at EY has been using to great effect – it's a great way of getting more introverted people to make a valuable contribution to the meeting.

✓ You might find it useful to run the group with all attendees standing up, as this improves brain function and the speed of the meeting.

✓ There is no such thing as a 'wrong' idea, as each thought could inspire another group member's thinking.

✓ The chair should make sure that everyone is contributing.

✓ Don't let the meeting go on longer than people are continuing to have inspiration. If the group is starting to flag, try reposing the problem with a slightly different question.

Questions can be more useful than answers. In an interesting *Harvard Business Review* article, Hal Gregersen shares the story of a brainstorming session that had run out of ideas.[5] Rather than waste the last 10 minutes, he asked everyone to think of the questions that they might want to answer in the next session. This then invigorated the debate, as the attendees engaged their minds in a different way. In doing so, it kick-started the whole discussion and led to far more fruitful results.

Walmart Gives Away Control

For their Oscars night ads in 2017, Walmart gave creative control to Hollywood directors Antoine Fuqua and Marc Forster, and Seth Rogen and Evan Goldberg. Each pair had to make a film based on a single Walmart receipt, reflecting the idea that 'every receipt tells a story'. The only guidance that the brand gave them was "be storytellers".

Appropriately for this chapter, Rogen and Goldberg's spot opens with a teacher writing "Finding Inspiration in Unusual Places" on the board, and saying, "Inspiration can be found anywhere if you really look for it." It then breaks into a musical number with a breadth of different products sung about by a scootering, roller-skating, dancing ensemble, as the camera moves seamlessly from scene to scene.

You can find a link to it on my website: www.newfirebook.com/links

Other ways of finding content ideas

✓ Ask your staff; they have a huge resource of life experience and insight on which to draw. You could create a competition that encourages people to come forwards with stories that you can share.

✓ Ask your customers; perhaps run a competition, and incentivise them with benefits and prizes.

✓ Social media provides you with a vast supply of stories and potential subjects. This has the added benefit of helping you to build your potential audience through finding the stories that you'll share.

✓ Utilise the charitable causes your business supports. This is a goldmine for potentially brilliant content. Speak to them, explain what you're trying to achieve and see what they might have to help you. As we covered in Chapter 4, though, it's important that you're playing an active role in supporting them before you start to use it in your marketing. Walk the walk before you talk the talk.

✓ Listen and be open minded; there are stories all around you. By keeping what you're trying to achieve in mind, you may be surprised how many potential story subjects you come across.

Focus groups and consensus creative

"If I had asked my customers what they wanted,
they would have said a faster horse."

– Henry Ford

Avoid the temptation to rely on focus groups for your creative thinking. As the saying goes, "A camel is a horse designed by a committee." Focus groups should only be used to test creative thinking with a given audience group.

Be bold with your creative ideas. Make sure they are grounded in research and audience understanding, and then allow the creatives to run with them. Choose your creative team/partners carefully, then back them. There is so much content shared online that you need to try to stand out. Creating content based on consensus will lead to work that is too 'vanilla' to really hit any specific audience. Focus groups lead to consensus, and consensus translates to no one getting what they wanted.

Testing, refining and reiterating creative

Instead, take time to understand the audience, their interests, their concerns and all the different elements outlined in their audience profiles. Once you have these, you should create three different ideas quickly and cheaply, and test them, either with your subscriber/membership group or with the wider market. This will give you a huge amount of data: how many people from which target groups watched which pieces of content, where did they drop off, were there any surprises in the data and so on. Once you have this information, you can share more content based on the learnings from the first tranche. You should continue this approach: reiterating, sharing and learning. All the while, you'll be gathering information that you can use to improve the effectiveness of your future content.

Creative confined

Corporate-film production has historically received a bit of a bad rap. At the glamorous end of the corporate-film world – advertising – there has always been an incentive to be as creative as possible. Corporate has languished in magnolia mediocrity because there has never been the incentive to create really great work. The audience was traditionally captive, because the audience was historically captive – they had to watch what was sent to them by head office.

One of the questions I get asked relatively often is how you can be creative when you're producing work to communicate dry financial or corporate messaging. The fact is that creativity without constraint is anarchy. By providing constraints, you actually make it easier, rather than harder, for creative thinking to flourish.

I illustrate this point in some of the presentations I give with the following two-stage thought experiment...

First, I want you to pause for a moment and try to think of something funny happening.

Now, I want you to think of something funny happening in a pie shop with a butcher and a chicken.

Hopefully, you should have found it significantly easier to think of something when I provided you with some constraints. There is nothing particularly funny, per se, about the aforementioned butcher and chicken in a pie shop, but it gave your mind something to work with.

How can you work with this fact? Make sure that the brief includes all the required information and stipulations, and then let the production team run with it.

We're all creative, really.

Keep an open mind

One of the great things about working as part of a filmmaking team is that you never know where a great idea will come from. It's the job of the director or producer to channel those thoughts into the final output. The same is true in a business setting. We all have the ability to be creative. We're conditioned by the modern education system to specialise from an early age. We're channelled to be artistic, good at maths and good at science. Of course, there are people to whom the principles of creativity come more naturally. From experience, it's often those with different backgrounds who are able to look at a problem from another angle, and share an idea or thought that the 'creatives' in the room might have overlooked. The importance of this approach to diverse thinking is reflected in the inclusion of art with STEM (science, technology, engineering and maths) to make it into STEAM.

We can illustrate our innate creativity with a simple thought experiment. Take an archetypal non-creative – the driest accountant, from the driest accounting job – and imagine them shipwrecked alone on a desert island. Within a few hours, they would have established a shelter in which to sleep and started to think about how they can gather food to eat. This is creativity in action; too many of us discount ourselves by saying that it isn't who we are.

Featuring Your Brand

Is it OK to feature your product and brand in the content that you produce? The answer is sometimes. One of the main goals of all the content that you create is to build trust with the audience and, through that, their affinity with your brand. You do this by offering them value – as much as possible. Of course, the goal is to massage your audience towards using your services, but that needs to happen in a fairly light-touch way. For example, if you're a shampoo brand, and you give your customer a rundown of the top ten hair products in your market and they're all yours, they're not going to feel that it is an objective piece of content to believe in. If you're very directly advertising a role in your company or a specific product as part of a sales-activation message (see page 95), then it is essential to feature your brand. Try to be balanced in tone, though, as sounding overly pushy will turn the audience off, even if you're directly trying to sell something. Illustrate the value the position/product offers, and make the sale based on that.

One thing to note on this is that if you are wanting to directly promote your brand, it's best to be really clear about this all the way through. According to the previously mentioned research by Dynamic Logic, intrigue doesn't really work. This is because you can't rely on the audience to stick around to see it. Because of this, you should get the brand in there and be clear about it. Similarly, creative that relies on a big reveal for impact can find it challenging to be effective. It cites highly entertaining ads as an exception to this rule.[6]

Choosing people to feature in your content

Unless you're creating an animation, you'll need to find some people to appear in your content. Most of the time, you'll want to feature your own employees in the content you produce. This gives you an opportunity to demonstrate the people and culture of the company. It can be nerve-wracking for someone to be on screen for the first time.

Three is the magic number

It's one of those things in life, but three is the magic number. It's the first prime number. It was a special number in ancient religions – prayer in salat are said three times, three wise men, the holy trinity, etc. It defines 'story', which we covered in Chapter 1: beginning, middle and end; past, present and future; and input, reaction and result. In speech and storytelling, working with triads gives far more impact to the delivery. It's the Goldilocks number for narrators – once is accident, twice is chance, three times is indisputable and four is too many.

Because of this, it's always useful to look for sets of threes when choosing the subjects of your videos. It keeps them balanced, which makes them significantly more watchable and digestible for the viewer. This, in turn, will increase the impact of your message. There can be a desire to fit more and more profiles into your films. The understanding being that if you're making the investment, you may as well cram as many people in front of the camera as possible.

The problem with this is that each featured individual needs space to breathe on screen. Just as in music, in film the silence or pauses can be as important as the sound. By not allowing the subjects space to 'be' on screen, the audience is overwhelmed by different characters, and never fully appreciates each subject for whom they are. This reduces the effect of the film overall. Have faith, and allow the subjects whom you've chosen to tell the broader story. What they lose in specificity, they will more than make up for in added engagement.

Actors vs 'real people'

Is it better to feature actors or 'real' people? It really depends on what you're trying to achieve and the logistics that you have available. The most important thing is that the performances feel genuine.

To that end, if you're documenting a role in your company, which is supposed to be the person who will play it in the film, it's best to work with the actual people involved.

If the role will require any acting – saying lines, reactions or anything beyond the simplest directions ('move here, look there'), I'd strongly recommend getting an actor.

Too often on shoots, the interviewees have written what they want to say or been given a script to regurgitate. They're not professional actors and this nearly always ends terribly. This particularly seems to affect more senior members of staff. They feel that more is at stake and that they are expected to perform at a certain level, which makes them even more nervous.

It's a lot better for the subjects to be briefed on the areas they are going to be interviewed about, to know their facts and then to have faith in themselves to stitch it all together on camera. I've always told interviewees that the crew are there to make them look good – that's their job and they've done it many, many times before. People get nervous about being interviewed because they are so used to seeing journalists on the news trying to catch out politicians. This isn't the way that this type of interview works.

In Summary: Getting the Right Creative Idea

Crafting a great creative idea is an essential step towards achieving results with your content. Make your content brilliant, and it will make any money you spend to promote it go many times further. In this chapter, we looked at some of the ways that you can come up with excellent, differentiating ideas. One of the best routes is nearly 80 years old (as follows).

A technique for producing ideas

✓ **Gather**… all the information that might be relevant to the project, including inspirations.

✓ **Think**… about all the different ways you could make the project work.

✓ **Forget**… about it, but try to keep it in the back of your mind.

✓ **Idea!**… An idea tends to pop into your head when you least expect it.

✓ **Craft**… your rough-diamond idea into a fit-for-purpose sparkler.

Brainstorms can be useful for getting everyone involved in the project to feel included from the outset. They do need to be run with discipline, though. Try allowing people who are more introverted to work in pairs, then feedback to the group to get the most from them.

Focus groups are good for testing the relevance of ideas to your target audience. *Don't* use them to come up with creative, though.

There are a number of other ways of finding good ideas. You need to keep an open mind, as they may come from anywhere. Once you've found a cracking idea, it's important that you test it and refine it to make it perfect.

Is it OK to *feature your brand* in your content marketing? The answer is sometimes. Bear in mind that the purpose of the majority of the content that you share should be to build trust with your audience by sharing content with them that they want to see. Once you've built that trust, then you can share sales messages. No one likes being sold to. Do it too much or too early, and you'll turn your audience off.

Should you feature *real people* or *actors* in your content? Always use real people if it's documentary-type content, and always use professional actors if the acting involved is anything more than very basic direction.

In the next chapter, we're going to look at how to find and tell excellent stories.

CHAPTER 10

HOW TO FIND AND TELL GREAT STORIES

As we saw in Chapter 1, stories are essential to how we understand the world around us. Story structure directly mirrors the way our brains have evolved to process and remember information. Every piece of content that you produce – no matter the length, the subject or the platform – should be a crafted piece of storytelling.

"Story, story, story."

That was how Sir Ridley Scott, one of the greatest living filmmakers, opened his address at the *New Directors' Showcase* at the Cannes Lions in 2018. There couldn't be a simpler encapsulation of the director's role in the filmmaking process. Great stories, well told, are essential to the effectiveness of video communication. Whether you're creating a feature-length drama or an animated learning module, you need to understand and use story structure. No matter what the purpose is, your content should follow the classic structure of beginning, middle and end.

The better your stories and the better the way they are told, the more effective your messaging; it's as simple as that.

Great stories clarify a message, making it more memorable and resonant to a wider audience than the same information poorly told. Therefore, you need to be able to find, recognise and relate excellent stories. Even if you're working with external producers, it's still important for you to know this, as you know your organisation far better than they can. You are key to them finding the best stories from within your business that you should be telling.

What Makes a Great Story

Great stories are all around us. The key to finding them is to be open minded. If you have a clearly defined purpose and you know how your products can be used to help/entertain people, you can start to think about the stories you can tell to bring this to life. With this in mind, there are a number of factors that you should look for in order to assess the impact of the stories you're looking to share. They should be the following (use the mnemonic CUBE to help you remember them):

>> **Clear**

>> **Unexpected**

>> **Believable**

>> **Emotive**

Clear

What are the core elements for the audience to understand? The best stories have a simple narrative and make sure that this is landed with the audience.

This is a famous story about a pitch process that British Rail ran in the 1970s. At the time, the company was seen as a joke. Its trains were always late, passenger numbers were dropping, its rolling stock was tired and aging, and it wasn't in a good place financially. It needed a new marketing campaign to remind the public what made it great.

The British Rail executives put out a tender for a new advertising agency. One well-known agency invited the British Rail team to visit its offices for its pitch. On arrival, the executives were met by a disdainful receptionist who did her utmost to ignore them, gesturing them into a waiting room full of litter, ashtrays overflowing with cigarette butts, and stained, dirty seats.

Five minutes passed. Then ten. After waiting for 15 minutes, the executives had finally had enough and angrily rose to leave. At that moment, the advertising team burst into the room and said to them, "That's how the public feels they are treated by you... Now, let's see what we can do to put it right."

They won the pitch.

This story shows us the importance of clarity. The advertising team could have given a presentation on the rich history of British Rail, it's culture, and how many trains it had or tonnage it moved. The agency stripped away everything and focused on the most significant pain point in the eyes of the customer. It was perfectly clear in its objective, and it didn't let anything get in the way of that.

Why does that matter to you? Well, whenever you're looking at a story to relate, try to work out what the most important elements are and then keep to these. Simplicity will make your story that much more likely to stick in the minds of the audience.

Don't be afraid of oversimplification. By far the greatest issue in corporate communications is not keeping it simple. This is particularly true if you're communicating about something that you have an in-depth knowledge of. The better we understand something, the more likely we are to not be able to explain it.

This can be illustrated by asking someone to drum 'Twinkle, Twinkle, Little Star' on the table. You then ask the next person to guess what they are drumming. Most people estimate that the percentage of people who will guess the right tune will be 50%. In reality, it's more like 2.5%. This is because the tapper can hear the notes of the tune in their head, while the guesser can't. Bear this in mind when explaining potentially complex things – such as your product.

Unexpected

We're constantly assaulted by so much information that our brains would go crazy if we tried to process it all. To deal with this, we're conditioned to tune out all but the most relevant information. It's estimated that the average American is subjected to 4,000 to 10,000 adverts or commercial messages every single day. How many do you remember from your last 24 hours? Very, very few, because you hardly even see them. For your story to be noticed, it must have an unexpected element to it. It must catch the audience member's eye, so that they switch off their autopilot and take notice of what you're saying.

Budweiser's 1995 'Bullfrogs' Super Bowl commercial is a great example of this. You don't see bullfrogs saying, "Bud... Weis... Er..." every day. Because of this, the audience took notice, remembered it and bought a lot of Budweiser's beer as a result. Look for the surprising in the stories you want to tell. It may just be a case of framing the story slightly differently to see it from an unusual angle. Whatever it is, it will make your story better and your message more impactful.

Believable

It goes without saying that the more believable a story is to the audience, the more likely it is to land its message. In dramatic storytelling, there is a degree of what is known as the 'willing suspension of disbelief'. All stories have a background of basic rules. The audience are willing overlook certain elements of the story that are flexing the plausible as long as the story doesn't break the established rules. This is why it's possible to tell extremely involving stories about made-up things, such as ghosts or aliens, without the audience dismissing them out of hand.

If the story is a documentary with a presenter, it's important to include people or information that underlines the believability of the points being made. What is the background of the person relating the story to the audience? Do they enter the story looking to discover the truth themselves, or are they in a position of knowledge and are informing the audience directly? Naturally, if you choose the latter, it's important that the presenter has the gravitas to carry it off.

Emotive

"The experience of the many, through the prism of the individual."

As a communicator, you're effectively operating a magnifying lens. You can choose where to point it to give the stories of individuals a greater standing than the stories of the many. As humans, we're unable to comprehend the experience of a mass of people, because there is too much complexity; it doesn't engage us emotionally. We find it harder to empathise with the experience of thousands than we do with that of one person. For that reason, you need to look for compelling stories of individuals, which can be used to reflect the story of the whole.

Humanity washed ashore

Think of the image of Alan Kurdi, the dead Syrian migrant boy on the Turkish beach. For months, the migrant crisis had rumbled on, with thousands of column inches devoted to stories of hundreds who drowned as their makeshift boats sank at sea. But it was in the one photo of the boy in the surf that the scale of the tragedy was brought home to the watching world. It turned statistics into something powerfully emotive.

I apologise for using such an affecting, negative example, but it really exemplifies this point. To tell really effective stories, you need to find the human experience that epitomises the wider message. You then need to humanise and personify the actors and forces within the story. The more real the characters and the more real the challenges they face, the more compelling their story will be to your audience.

Robert Capa

"If your photographs aren't good enough, you're not close enough."
– Robert Capa

As a teenager, before mobile phones, I used to travel everywhere with a camera. I'd take photos of the things that caught my eye. Most of all, somewhat macabrely, I was ready for a major incident, a terrorist-bomb attack or maybe a car crash. I was ready to capture the news. I had decided that I wanted to be a war photographer. I wanted to capture the experience of life lived at the very edge, and to experience the limits of the human condition, both positive and negative. One of my great heroes was the Hungarian-born World War II photographer Robert Capa. He captured all of the romance, swagger and adventure that made it such a compelling career for a risk-taking teenager. He was the only photographer to go ashore with Allied troops in the landing craft on D-Day.

The previous quotation is essential for anyone looking to become a better storyteller. Of course, there is the physical truth of what he is saying. Most people's photos would benefit from taking a couple of steps towards the subject – just ask any passing stranger to take a photo of you and your family. But, then, there is the metaphysical truth: great photos, and great stories, come from a closeness and a familiarity with the subject. If the stories you're looking to tell aren't good enough, if you lack the details that make a story really sing for the audience, then you need to get closer to the subject. The video you're creating needs more of the almost imperceptible touches of humanity, which bring them to life.

Other things to think about when choosing a story...

The first step is to be clear about what you're trying to communicate.

You can get there by thinking about what you're trying to achieve:

» **Who are the target audience? How might this change the subject/ focus of your content?**

» **What is the key message you're trying to get across? What is the action that you're trying to inspire in the audience?**

» **Video is an emotive medium, so how will the emotion you generate influence the audience to take the desired action – even if it's just watching the next video in the series?**

» **Do you have a specific call to action (CTA) at the end of the film?** Bear in mind the fact that you need to build affinity with the audience through providing videos they like before you put across a pointed sales message. More detail is given on CTAs shortly.

» **What is the tone of voice of your story going to be?** This may change the subject that you want to focus on.

» **What are the final outputs of the video going to be?** The content you focus on for a single feature-length documentary will probably be very different from what it would be if you were producing a large number of short-form mini-documentaries for Snapchat.

» **How many outputs do you think you'll need?** Is this a one-off, or do you need to find a series of subjects that could make up an ongoing series?

How to Define the Central Message/moral

Before you begin, it's important to think about what message you're trying to relay. The more focused you can be with this the better, so try to boil it down to a single message or moral. This significantly increases the chance of your message landing. All the best films have a very clear message at the heart of them, such as 'Guinness Surfers' – exhilaration that is worth waiting for – and *Jurassic Park* – beware men playing God – is another good example. Avoid the temptation to muddy the waters by trying to include more than one message in any video that you make. If you have more than one message, make another video or even series of videos to illustrate that.

Once you have this clear in your mind, think about how you can use the different potential tools and subjects you have to bring them to life. Every single thing that you do from here on should be in the service of relaying this message. This will include the actors, script, locations, camera/production equipment and edit style – everything. If you do this, it will make the film clear and impactful. This is particularly important in the online/multiple-screen environment in which your content will be watched. If it can make sense to people who are only half paying attention, then you're well on your way to landing your message with the wider audience.

The challenge to be overcome

"A movie is only ever as good as its villain."
– Alfred Hitchcock

As we explored in Chapter 1, great stories rely on the exposition of a genuine challenge to be overcome. Whether Hitchcock said the aforementioned quotation or not, what it means is that a story is only ever as good as the personification of the antagonist/challenge that faces the protagonist/main character. The key, then, to telling great stories lies in the ability of the storyteller to make the different elements of the story real for the audience. We need to wholly believe in the authenticity of the protagonist; we need to believe in the tension that lies between them and the achievement of their goal.

I understand that you might be reading this and thinking, *This sounds very theoretical, what on earth do protagonists and antagonists have to do with getting my graduate interns to watch a talking-head video about topping up their company pensions?* Well, this is because understanding it will help you to make films that they will want to watch and will remember the content of. Taking that example, let's look at how we can break it down.

The traditional corporate-video approach to this might just be to outline the facts in a voiceover, with the information written up on the screen: "If you pay in x now, you'll have y in the future. If you top up to 2x, you might have 4y in the future." This might be compelling to an accountant, but it won't have the same impact as really bringing the different elements of the story to life. The protagonist in this story might be someone in the same position as the audience. The antagonist is a future without an adequate pension. So far, so obvious.

In order to do this, we might choose to have two characters who work together – Sarah and Bill. As a storyteller, we want to make them personable, so we show a little of their lives, with some small details that help humanise them: Sarah loves coffee, but only with two sugars, and Bill loves travelling to see new places.

Sarah decides to top up her pension payments, while Bill doesn't – he has to save what he can to travel. Sarah knows that the cost of doing that is the coffee that she normally has on the way into work. She grabs one in the office instead. Over time, thanks to the magic of compound interest, those cups of coffee really add up. By the time she retires, she can afford trips to Guatemala to see her favourite coffee growing. Bill, unfortunately, doesn't top up his pension, which means that he is left with a very basic pay out. It means that he can't afford to travel any more. Sarah is nice enough to send him a postcard, though.

That's a pretty simple example, but it does show how building a little more depth into the story and the characters makes it more effective and compelling.

Next time you watch an advert or piece of visual storytelling, keep an eye out for how the filmmakers humanise the characters. It could be in the simplest, shortest spot, but there will probably still be a tiny touch – a look or expression – which aims to build a connection between the audience and the characters.

In order to tell great stories with video, you need to look for ways of humanising your subjects. The more effectively and believably you do this, the more effective your films will be in capturing the audience's attention and generating memory-forming emotions.

The call to action (CTA)

Whatever you want the audience to do as a result of watching the video, it's best to actually ask them to do it.

The CTA should be simple, clear and create a sense of urgency. Sometimes it's best to have it at the end, but at other times you may get a better response from placing it earlier in the video. As you can see from figure 13, (page 204) hosting platform Wistia reports a significant drop-off in the last 15 seconds of any video, so make sure that your viewers are actually getting to see it. The fantastically successful Dollar Shave Club's CTA, pops up 10 seconds into their video.

The key thing with CTAs, as with much of the online-video process, is that you should always A/B test* and optimise. Try experimenting with different ones, and then focus on the ones that work for your target audience.

---

* See Going Viral on page 234 for tips on A/B testing

In Summary: How to Find and Tell Great Stories

As we saw at the beginning of the book, stories directly mirror the way the human brain interprets and remembers information. The ability to recognise and relate great stories is essential to making the most of your video communications. The better the storytelling, the more powerful the emotive effect, and the more likely your audience are to remember and act on it – which is what we're after.

A good way of thinking about *what makes a good story* is to use the mnemonic CUBE.

Clear

What does the audience need to know to land the message? Limit the information that you include to that which directly benefits the story. Also, ensure that all the techniques that are used aid the understanding and impact of the message.

Unexpected

To cope with the vast amount of information that constantly assaults our senses, our brains filter out all the information that it deems unnecessary. Information that is out of the ordinary jolts the audience out of autopilot, making the story more engaging.

Believable

This is a pretty obvious one, but the best stories need to be plausible. Even if it's the most fantastical tale, once you've established the 'rules' of the environment in which it's set, you must not break them.

Emotive

Video is the emotive medium. Look for stories that naturally engage your audience's hearts. Your audience are far more susceptible to emotive stories of individuals, from which they can extrapolate the experience of the whole, than they are to simply the story of the whole.

There are a number of other things that might affect what you choose to relate as a story. These include the target audience, the action that you're trying to inspire, the tone and the CTA. Whatever you choose, it's important to consider what the central truth or moral you're communicating is. Make sure that this is illustrated as clearly as possible by the subject of your story and the way it's told.

As we examined in Chapter 1, all stories are about a degree of conflict or jeopardy. The greater the jeopardy, the more compelling the story. If you can add jeopardy or conflict – even just a tiny amount – your stories will be more interesting to your audience.

The point of telling great stories is to engage your audience enough that they will then go on and do something else. You're aiming to drive an action. Because of this, it's best to ask them to do it. This is the CTA. Don't forget to include one in your video, even if you're just asking people to subscribe using a graphic strap in the bottom corner.

In the next chapter, we'll look at the importance of data and how to use it.

CHAPTER 11

USING DATA TO INFORM CONTENT

"The biggest difference between Don Draper and now is data."
– Keith Weed, Chief Marketing and Communications Officer, Unilever[1]

Not long ago, to get any kind of information on a target market, marketers needed to send out surveys or run focus groups. This made the process extremely heavy. For example, the census that the US government runs every 10 years takes several years to compile. This means that all the information it contains is out of date before anyone gets their hands on the latest copy. This has all changed now that the number of smart devices in circulation has exploded. We track how many steps we take, the places we visit and web searches without trying. There is also a huge amount of data accessible to video marketers. We can use this to create content that we know your target audience will want to engage with. This makes the understanding and use of data an extremely important tool for video marketers.

Netflix, House of Cards and Big Data

Netflix shows just how far companies can go when using data to inform the types of content it shares. Its flagship series, *House of Cards*, is a massive hit with its subscribers, with 86% saying that they were less likely to cancel their subscription because of the show, according to a survey by Cowan and Company. Back in 2011, the company took the massive step of commissioning two series of the show in one go, 26 episodes, for over US$100 million – US$3.8 million an episode, without seeing a single one![2]

Is that bravery or foolhardiness? It was actually a careful calculation based on big data. Before making the decision, it knew a number of key relevant facts about its users:

» A significant number of users had watched the whole of the David Fincher directed movie *The Social Network*.

» The original British version of *House of Cards* had been well watched.

» People who watched the British version of *House of Cards* also watched Kevin Spacey films and/or films directed by David Fincher.

This allowed it to make a judgement call that the new series was worth its investment. Having this information also allows it to target users with other content that they might like. It's also able to see who is at risk of giving up their subscription by seeing how much they have been using it over the past month.

Why does this matter to you?

Obviously, Netflix is in a strong position as it's able to directly track how its subscribers access its services on a person-by-person basis. There are ways that you can use data without having quite such an in-depth view, though. For example, A/B testing a number of different creative treatments/video names/thumbnail images before choosing the one that resonates most successfully with our audience is a form of data optimisation we should all be doing.

Beyond this, you can see in greater depth than you might at first glance. You have access to a surprising amount of data if you choose to. Many of the clients I've worked with in the past haven't been able to make the most of the data they could be collecting. This is usually because of concerns around hosting and data security. There are some very powerful platforms that can host video securely, giving access to in-depth information, but it requires the clients making a choice to utilise them. This has been an argument that we've lost more often than not.

Given this fact and the natural limitations that you'll have when you first start using data, it's important that you don't give up on the experience and intuition of your team/suppliers. Data can provide a grounding for decisions, but it's important that you weigh the information up and make a rational choice based on what you have. Data can give you the insight that will help you to optimise your product and improve your value proposition. You just need to look at what you have access to and how this can help you.

Qual vs Quant

The majority of the information that is accessible from online video platforms is quantitative (quant); i.e. it tracks the number of people taking each action. The benefit of this is that it's extremely light touch as far as the audience are concerned – it happens without them realising it's happening. What it isn't so good at is qualitative (qual) analysis; i.e. assessing the quality of each interaction. The traditional methods of getting this information still exist – focus groups and forms – but the challenge with these is that people don't always say what they really think. Also, if you have a form for the audience to fill in at the end of any piece of communication, you must bear in mind that it becomes part of the communication, and may limit or change the action they take as a result.

Oath (Yahoo!) Storytellers and Chevrolet - Case study

As the number of data points available to content commissioners increases, they are able to use the data points to make ever-more-insightful observations about the types of content you should be producing for a given audience. This is particularly true for businesses – such as publishers (The Wall Street Journal, Condé Nast, CNN, etc.) – that have built up a wealth of data from the past work that they have shared.

Take Oath – formerly Yahoo! – for example. It has over a billion monthly users. Each of those users' actions is tracked, which builds up a picture of their online habits. Oath suggests that it receives and records 4 trillion data signals per month.[3] This breadth of information allows it to judge what will and won't be successful for certain demographics.

For example, Oath's content studio was commissioned to produce a series to promote family cars for Chrysler. From its data, it was able to tell that, of its users who were in the market for a family car, 51% were female, 73% were married and 70% had children. It also knew that millennial parents/ expecting parents using Oath were 46% more likely to agree that they like the same products that celebrities use. It also knew that comedy was their favourite genre. Through all of this information, it was able to understand the type of content that would work best for the target audience, and create a series of comedy in-car interviews called *Going There with Anna Gasteyer*. Supporting this, it had a digital site with a variety of supporting content aimed at enticing mums, based on the search terms it knew they used. This led to increases in the click-through rate (+33%), purchase intent (+6%) and brand trust (+5%) among the target audience.[4]

Challenges to Data

The quality of the decisions you're able to make as a result of a piece of data is only ever going to be as good or reliable as the underlying data itself. Because of this, you need make sure that you can trust all of the data that you include. As we'll see, the seemingly unstoppable rise of data has, to an extent, been checked by a number of setbacks.

Shortcomings with data-led creative

There are a few shortcomings of the data-led approach, which mean that those nice luvvies in the creative department shouldn't be sweating too much just yet. Firstly, while all that data can undoubtedly be used to improve the background understanding that informs a creative idea, the information still needs human creative thought to establish the idea itself. Secondly, by becoming too data-centric, there is a danger that you end up travelling down a creative rabbit hole, only ever producing variations on the same work you've done in the past, because that's where your best/safest dataset is. Finally, you need to be certain that the data is telling you what you think it is. For example, the most commonly tracked video data is views and engagements – shares, likes and comments. While it might be good for your self-esteem to know that your video has had over 1 million views since you shared it, it's not going to help with your strategy if all of those people are either bots or from the wrong target group. The more trustworthy detail that you can get, the more useful data will be as a tool.

DATA IS REALLY USEFUL, UP TO A POINT, BUT YOU DO NEED TO USE IT SENSIBLY

Putting a number on emotion: Realeyes - Case Study

Realeyes is one of the most interesting platforms that I've seen in this space. This uses facial-expression-recognition software to judge engagement among a specific audience while watching different types of content. It has a wide-ranging focus group based all over the world. The platform then shares specific videos with the viewer, and records and rates them against the six basic facial expressions: happiness, surprise, sadness, disgust, fear and confusion. These emotions look the same no matter where in the world the person exhibiting them is from. It did look at including anger, but it found that people are practically never outwardly angry towards ads. The platform then takes this information and makes its own judgements, which are net positive, net negative and engagement. Engagement is the level of reaction the video generated, second to second, as it played. The system is then able to provide a second-by-second emotional score for the film, tracking engagement and allowing the production team to understand where it's losing the viewers' attention. This then allows it to make changes to the production to remedy the issues.

Where this software gets really interesting, for our purposes, is in the fact that it can judge how successful a piece of content will be before it's even shared. At the minute, running the system is too expensive to work for basic online videos. However, it's only a matter of time before it calculates how to run the system without the expensive/time-consuming element of the focus group.

Beware of the Bots

You need to be aware of ad fraud – it can significantly impact the quality of the information you get and potentially cost you a lot. Bots allow hackers to take over computers and then use them to automatically view adverts, creating huge amounts of fake traffic and earning the hackers advertising dollars. Bots were expected to cost advertisers $19 billion in 2018, which is a number that is set to rise to US $44 billion by 2022.[5] Beyond this significant cost is that fact that they make a lot of the information online untrustworthy. The 'zombie' computers that the bots create can appear to be anywhere geographically. The personas of the people supposedly using them are not only worthless but could prompt you into decisions based on false information.

This makes it even more important to use methods of data gathering that are rooted in real-audience insight. This could be focus groups, customer surveys/conversations, or interactions by users that you've been able to certify.

Data-protection Regulation

It's become a bit of an Internet-age truism, but – as they say – if you don't have to pay for it, you are the product. As trust in social media platforms has taken a bit of hit in recent years, there has been growing concern about the amount of our data that companies save, access and use. This has led to steps by governments to curb this power. The most famous of these has been the General Data Protection Regulation (GDPR), which came into effect in the EU in May 2018. This has been designed to place restrictions on data storage and usage, and carries some fairly hefty penalties for those who misuse it.

This regulation has had a chilling effect on the way that many businesses engage with potential customers, with most businesses choosing to play it safe rather than be made an early scapegoat. This is particularly relevant, as it stipulates that European citizens are protected whether they are in the EU or not. This has spread the concern further afield. There will, no doubt, be further regulations over the coming years, as governments get to grips with how to control and counter the vast monopolies that the digital world has spawned. This makes it even more important that you're producing the kind of content that your audience want to see in their inboxes.

In Summary: Data

Data is an extremely valuable tool for video marketers. The real value becomes apparent when you're able to move beyond the more basic information – views, likes and shares – and look at how your target audience interacts with the content you produce. This allows you to optimise your content, potentially making films that you *know* your target market will watch.

As with most tools, as useful as data can be in helping you to make decisions, it needs to be used with experience and intuition to maximise on its benefits. There are some things to bear in mind before you start putting too much store in the benefits of data. The amount that we're able to gather and use has been curtailed by government-enforced data protection – GDPR in Europe, which is for European citizens all over the world. The quality of data can also be damaged by the erroneous noise created by bots.

CHAPTER 12

THE OPTIMAL LENGTH FOR ONLINE VIDEOS

"What's the best length for online video?" is a very common question with, on the face of it, a relatively simple answer: short. Beyond that, though, it gets a little bit more complicated. To begin with, there are a few rules of thumb:

» You have 6 seconds to capture the viewers' attention. YouTube's pre-roll ads can be closed after 12 seconds, for instance, so you have to work fast.

» By 30 seconds you'll have lost 33% of the audience.

» By 1 minute you'll have lost 45% of the audience.

» By 2 minutes you'll have lost 60% of the audience.

"Drama is life with the boring bits taken out."
– Alfred Hitchcock

To the uninitiated, this seems like not much time. In reality, video has the effect of compressing time, which means you can include a surprising amount of story/content in just a few seconds. This is because, as Hitchcock alludes in the previous quotation, you remove everything that doesn't add directly to the message/story.*

The length of the video itself will also have an effect on how far through viewers are likely to get. You can see this from the following graph of the viewer drop-off rate by video-hosting platform Wistia.

This makes the brilliantly economic use of language that is the writing of Ernest Hemmingway a valuable area of study/reading for those interested in enhancing their short-filmmaking abilities.

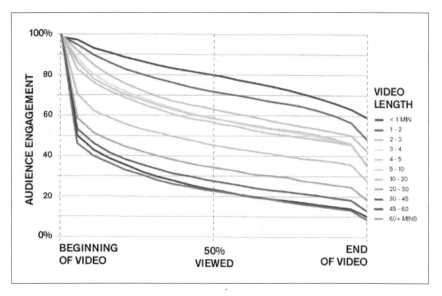

Figure 13. Wistia's analysis of audience engagement vs video length on their video sharing site

There are a couple of things to take from the previous graph. The first is the rapid drop-off rate in the first and last 5% of the viewing time. This means that you need to focus on making the opening section of your content as good as possible to hook the audience. It also means that if you have a CTA as part of the video, you need to make sure that you don't leave it to the end frame. Ideally, you need to try to work it in during the opening moments.

The second point is that if you want the audience to experience the majority of your content, you need to make it short. Many viewers won't even click on a video that they can see is longer than they want to invest in it. Figures for these avoiders are obviously not recorded in this graph. Having been watching, studying and sitting on awards panels for corporate videos for over a decade, I'm sorry to say that most of them could benefit from losing 10–25% of their length. Too often, producers get carried away with their own creations, or commissioners squeeze in just a little too much messaging and the 'Sin of Flabbiness' becomes unavoidable.

I don't mean this to contradict my belief that we're currently enduring the 'Tyranny of Brevity' online. Social media algorithms are designed to keep the user scrolling, and always chasing the next endorphin micro-hit, but never quite satisfying their desire. This has made attention spans shorter, which means that the content has to match it to keep up. There has been an ongoing drive towards ever shorter outputs, to the point now where Facebook regards any part of the video screen being viewable on the browser for longer than two seconds as a view. That's obviously starting to push the limits of plausibility. There is a fightback underway, though, as audiences seek out a deeper understanding of an increasingly confusing world – as shown by the success of 1-hour-long+ podcasts and Netflix documentaries. *Make it good, and people will watch it.*

There's a little more to it than that, though…

Factors Determining the 'Right' Video Length

"Nearly two-thirds of consumers prefer video under 60 seconds."

– Animoto[1]

The content of the video

There are many different types of content to share online (see Chapter 3). The audience will invest their time in the different types in different ways, depending on what they are looking to get out of them. For example, an amusing cat video promo will lose its appeal pretty quickly, whereas an in-depth look into your company's culture and induction process will hold a potential new recruit's attention as long as it takes. Generally, if you're sharing knowledge – learning and development, or a documentary – then you can afford to be a bit longer. If you get above three or four minutes, though, you might want to split it into parts. However, quality still wins: the excellent TED talks get millions of views and many of them are over 15 minutes in length.

The quality of the creative messaging/pacing

Time is relative. This is why a well-paced, 7,200-second (2-hour) feature film can flash by, but an annoying, 12-second pre-roll you didn't ask for seems like it goes on for ever. Anyone who has watched a loving aunt's shaky, full, unedited coverage of a wedding has glimpsed the true meaning of eternity. The way the video is made plays a significant role in the level of engagement you can expect from the audience. Is watching a pleasurable thing to do or does it jar in a way that doesn't drive the narrative? Poorly mastered sound – with loud pops, intrusive music and inaudible dialogue – is a killer.

Good pacing isn't necessarily about the action taking place quickly – pacing can be slow and still be right; its another element of film grammar, and so needs to be appropriate to serve the narrative. The bottom line is that you want to keep the pacing snappy.

Two Simple Steps to Better-quality Video

The number-one and two giveaways of amateur filmmaking are poor-quality audio and lighting. If you can get these two things right, you're hot on Coppola's heels. As I've already mentioned, this book isn't about the hands-on skills – there are hundreds of YouTube videos on the subject. Here are two small tips, though:

✓ Always, always, always monitor the audio going into the camera/recorder – some simple earphones will allow you to do this. You wouldn't shoot film without looking at the screen, so don't record audio without checking it's OK. Shooting in offices is blighted by air conditioning. Get it turned off or move away. Yes, it *will* matter. If you must have additional background audio, or 'noises off', try to film the source or include it in the shot so that the audience knows where the sound is coming from.

✓ Modern cameras have far better dynamic range (the ability to record extremes of light and dark) than they used to. This makes them more forgiving in less experienced hands. They still work best with plenty of light though. The fundamental lighting set-up incorporates three light sources. The 'primary' light source is the main illumination for the subject. The 'back light' gives a subtle wrap around the edge of the subject from behind, helping to distinguish them from the background. The 'fill light' softens any shadows from the 'primary' light. It's best if the 'fill' is less intense than the 'primary' light as having directional lighting is more aesthetically pleasing. Try moving the light sources around to see how it effects the look of the image. It's more flattering to have the 'primary' light more in line with the camera, whereas having it more off to the side will make the subject's features more pronounced/dramatic. It is also worth using a 'diffuser' on the light to soften them, reducing the starkness of shadows and making the lighting appear less artificial.

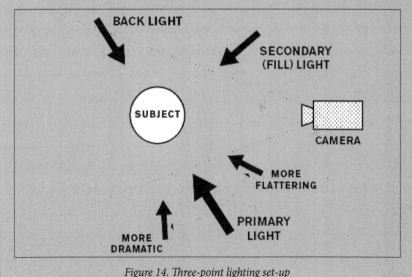

Figure 14. Three-point lighting set-up

Viewer expectations of the content

The frame of mind of the viewer makes a difference too. Netflix's videos are generally consumed sitting on a sofa, with remote in hand. The audience sit down ready to invest the time in something potentially substantial. Their frame of reference here is traditional TV/DVD movies, so the expectation is for content to last longer. If you're sharing to the audience's Facebook feed, then they expect it to be fairly short, so will be less willing to invest time in a longer video.

The device the audience are using

Where the viewer is watching the video also impacts how long they are willing to watch for. Obviously, if the audience have travelled to a cinema, they have made the decision to invest an evening of their time in your film – as the phenomenal success of *The Lego Movie* proved. When they are watching on their mobile device, on a packed train or bus, scrolling through a never-ending feed of content, you're going to need something seriously impressive and fast to catch their attention. Between these two extremes lies sitting on the sofa/couch watching on their TV, then their laptop, then their mobile. This is roughly defined by how easy it is for the viewer to navigate away from the content – on the phone, it's just a few degrees of thumb movement.

Whether the content is optimised for the platform/device

Making sure the content is formatted to make the most of the device/platform will help to increase engagement. For example, framing the video as portrait/square for mobile and landscape for desktop/connected TV makes a big difference. We've found that we can expect an increase in viewing time by 400% via framing in mobile-compatible portrait orientation.

It used to be that viewers would save content until they could watch it on a suitable device. Longer-form films would be watched on their connected TV/laptop, and snackable content would generally be watched as it was received on their mobile device. This has shifted over the last three years to the point where the best screen to watch on is the one closest to hand. This trend has increased the amount of video watched on mobile devices. This trend is being accelerated by the widescale uptake of 4G, followed by 5G, which is still to come. This means that mobile video is coming of age. It also means that it's essential that all video is optimised for mobile devices

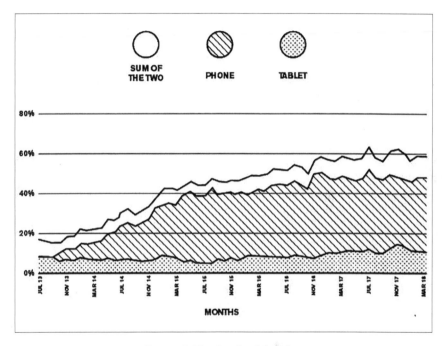

Figure 15. The rise of mobile video

The social platform it's being viewed on

Users interact with different social platforms in different ways. The content you create needs to match the style in which they use each one, as detailed in the following sections. This means that you need to tailor your video to the platform you'll be sharing it on. No matter what the platform, the first six to 12 seconds are absolutely essential. Don't make the mistake of filling this valuable time with a logo – it wastes the opportunity to hook the audience.

If you're restricted to a shorter video, it's best to use it to intrigue the viewer into clicking through to a platform that favours longer-form videos, where you can share more information.

Instagram

The endless scroll of images on Instagram means that the audience is extremely transient, scrolling almost without seeing. This means you need to work fast and be visually impactful to hook them: 30 seconds is the maximum length. The most-commented-on videos on Instagram are 26 seconds long.[2] We've had the most success with 15-second videos, shot in portrait.

Twitter

Twitter is another platform where the audience have a bitesize mindset, so it's best to be short. The absence of the continuous scroll, and the fact that the audience are reading rather than looking at images (which the brain processes far faster) means you have a little more time. While the maximum length is 2:20 minutes (or 140 seconds – see what they did there?), the average #VideooftheDay is 43 seconds in length. Once again, I'd recommend sticking to 45 seconds as the maximum.

Facebook

The maximum recommended length for Facebook is around one minute. Again, this is fairly short, but it's enough time to tell a story that's compelling enough to prompt the viewer to want to find out more.

With Facebook Stories – the Snapchat-style videos that disappear after 24 hours – the maximum video length is 20 seconds.

The maximum length for a Facebook Live broadcast is a whopping 240 minutes. With live broadcasting, you tend to pick up viewers as you go, so longer becomes better for increasing engagement.

YouTube

YouTube is the king of online video platforms. It's set up for watching high-quality video, and the audience go there with the specific intention of engaging with video content. This means that your videos can be longer still, up to around 2 to 2:30 minutes in length. If you have more content than this, try 'chunking' or splitting it into shorter pieces.

LinkedIn

LinkedIn has a very high proportion of mobile users; this means that content should be around 90 seconds in length and optimised for mobile users.

Your homepage

It's really useful to have a video on your homepage, as it allows the visitor to quickly identify what you do and what's special about the way that you do it. It brings the nature of your business to life. Because you're trying to hook them into finding out more, it's important that this is pretty snappy, so, ideally, it should be around 1 minute in length and not more than 1:30.

Your company's product pages

Once the audience have clicked through to your product pages, they have made a decision to find out more. This means that the content here should be a bit more informative. This means that you can afford to include more content, pushing the ideal length to around two to three minutes.

Your company's careers page

Visitors to your careers page are looking to find out two things: Firstly, do I like the look of the culture/people/opportunities? And, secondly, can I get any information about the job that might help me make a decision/apply?

In answering the first of these questions, it's best to keep the videos short. They should be exciting employer brand videos of not more than 90 seconds in length. For those looking for more information, you can afford to offer a bit more, with an average video being around three minutes and not more than five minutes in length.

In Summary: The Optimal Length for Online Videos

Video has the effect of compressing time. Because of this, you'd be surprised how much information you can get into even a short video. This is lucky because – generally, for online content – the shorter the content, the better.

There are a few things to bear in mind when considering how much of a piece of content your audience will watch. This is important because you want to share content at a length and in a format that the audience will consume in its entirety.

The content of the video

Your audience are more likely to invest time in something that they need to know – a training video, for example – than something that they see as less useful or that offers them less value.

The quality of the creative messaging/pacing

People are far more likely to invest their time in something that is well made and well paced. This is why millions of people are willing to spend scores of hours watching boxsets.

The viewers' expectations of the content

What are the audience expecting? In the boxset example, they may have just got some pizza in and are sitting down to spend the evening watching. The same is not the case for some click-bait that caught their eye while they were waiting for a bus.

The device they are watching it on

This ties in to the previous point. The length of time people are watching content for on mobile devices is actually increasing, aided by faster data connections. Generally, though, they are more likely to watch longer-form content on a connected TV and shorter content on their mobile device.

Whether the content is optimised for the platform/device

The content you share should be optimised for the device that it's destined for. Device-wise, that means mobile, as that is where the majority of viewing takes place. For platforms, bear in mind that social media platforms tend to play video without audio until the viewer chooses to turn the sound on. This means that you should use subtitles to increase engagement/comprehension.

The platform it's being hosted on

There are differences in the amount of time the audience will view content for between platforms. Instagram's infinite-scroll function leads to a very short engagement, but YouTube's video-centred configuration leads to longer watch times.

In the next chapter, we'll look at how to choose the right route to get your content produced.

CHAPTER 13

CHOOSING THE RIGHT PARTNER – AGENCY/INTERNAL/FREELANCE

I should probably declare a fairly healthy interest in you going down the content-agency route. Doing all the exciting things in this book is exactly what Casual does. I naturally look on the production-company/agency approach favourably, because, as a sector, we do great work (Particularly Casual, but I would say that). That said, I've tried to be as objective as I can. There is no perfect route. You need to meet some of the people who can provide for your needs, and work out if you trust them to deliver the best solution for you.

Having decided on everything else, it's now time to decide who is actually going to produce your project. This book has given you an overview of the processes and thinking that go into creating effective corporate/brand video. While I'm sure you could now head off and start shooting, this book is meant for those who'll work with others to get the most from the medium.

The next big question to answer, then, is *who might those others might be?* They fall into three distinct camps, each with their own strengths and weaknesses:

1. An external agency
2. Internal resources
3. Freelancers

Working with an External Agency

Simply put, if you want the very best return from your content, you need to be prepared to invest in it. This will lead you to look out a content agency or even to go through an advertising agency. The benefit of this is that you're working with professionals who can guide you through the whole process. They will have worked with a wide range of businesses like yours, and understand how to use content to engage an audience and achieve the key performance indicators (KPIs) that you're after. They also will have the scale that allows them to employ specialists in each area of the process, which means that you get the best people in each job.

You'll get a producer or account manager who'll do a lot of the organising for you. It also means that if there are any challenges to the production, you'll have someone to kick (proverbially, obviously!) to put it right.

The downsides of taking this approach are that agencies have their own overheads that they have to cover, so they will charge a premium on the price of the production staff. This makes this approach more expensive than some of the others that are available. Another issue is that you may find that you need to manage and consolidate work across a number of different suppliers, as each agency may be a specialist in a given area, but not another, or may lack the capability to give you exactly what you need.

Advertising Agencies

Advertising agencies have had a rough time over the last few years, as more and more clients have looked at their significant fees and asked whether they can really be justified. Before the technological advances detailed earlier in the book, they were able to charge handsomely for the quality of their thinking and oversight of the process. The problem now is that so much content is small in scale and needs to be turned around so quickly that it can be very difficult for them to add the value that they used to. I know that a client of ours once spent £100K on a single film with a large advertising agency. When it came back and he could see that it clearly wasn't £100K worth of film, he demanded to know exactly how much the production company had been paid to make it. They had got £20K, and they had done the creative and scripted it. The agency had effectively pocketed £80K for the introduction. Stories like this have been extremely damaging to the industry.

This isn't to say that there isn't a huge amount of extremely high-quality thinking, strategy and creative that happens in them, you just need to be selective in how you use them. Many production companies are used to working direct to client now, so can offer much of the same creative and business understanding. They aren't as good at the overarching concept, though – ad agencies can still be worth it if you have a lot of money to get it right.

Working with Internal Resources

There has recently been a real drive to bring video production in house and use an internal team to produce work. There are a number of reasons for doing this. They are part of the company and so it can lead to significant cost savings. They also understand and are invested in the brand, which should lead to a better, more consistent output. With video production being far more accessible than before, it makes it very easy for a company to employ their own producers and filmmakers to create the work that they need. At Casual, we work with a wide range of internal filmmaking resources. Some of them are lone filmmakers, others are vast multimillion-dollar studios with the permanent teams to manage them. Much of their output is really excellent.

There are some potential problems with taking this approach, though. One of the good things about using external producers is that they can offer a more objective viewpoint on what you're creating. For example, it seems less likely that an external agency would have been as susceptible to 'groupthink' as the internal Pepsi team who came up with the disastrous Kendall Jenner ad (see box on page 116).

External suppliers can also be kept a tiny bit hungry – by turning the tap on and off as you feel their interest ebbing and flowing – which means that you're more likely to be able to get them to go the extra mile. Internal teams are going to get the work whether or not they do it well and are keen, so there is far less impetus for the discretionary effort that really makes a project sparkle. This is particularly true for work that might be considered less desirable in the first place. This can make using internal resources not quite as cheap as it might first appear. There is nothing more expensive than someone who doesn't do the work you need them to. Then, there are the indirect costs of employment and additional headcount. This leads to the classic in-house/external merry-go-round, which most companies that go down this route engage in:

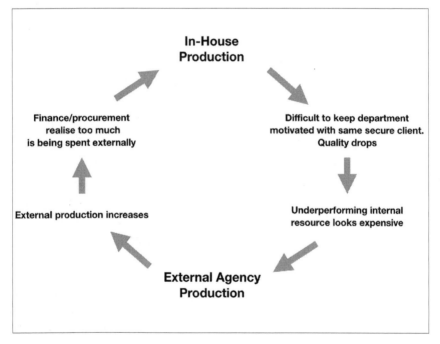

Figure 16. The internal/external video-supplier merry-go-round

Working with Freelancers

Finally, you may choose to act as your own executive producer, and hire in your own freelance talent. This has the benefit of potentially saving you a tidy sum, and it means that you won't have to add headcount into your department or company to do it. There are some really excellent filmmakers out there, and if you find a good producer, the chances are that they will be able to manage the whole process for you.

There are some significant potential pitfalls here, though. You run the risk of things not going to plan, and you being left 'holding the baby' as a result. Because of this, it helps if you know what you're doing if you want to go down this route. If you're working with an individual, there is the possibility that they may fall ill at a key moment, which is something that a larger resource will insulate you against.

It's surprising how deft certain freelancers can be at blinding their employers with the science of video production. Crashed renders, upload times and corrupted disks are all part of the arsenal that is deployed to explain delays and shortcomings. That isn't to say that these won't sometimes be true, it's just that it helps to know what they're talking about, so you can call them out when appropriate.

Freelancer networks

There are a number of networks of freelancers that will take your brief and then share it. As a commissioner, you get to choose the approach that you feel works best, and then the production goes from there. These have many of the benefits of working with freelancers – cost reductions, and access to a breadth of talent and ideas – but aren't without risks. The networks often offer little in the way of security in terms of the product. As you're effectively choosing an individual – admittedly, the one who comes across best in their pitch – you may find that the reduction in cost comes at a far greater price.

In Summary: Choosing the Right Partner

As with all things in life – apart from the best things, which are, of course, free – you get what you pay for. You need to assess what you're trying to achieve and then resource it as required. If you want to create a basic event film of an internal event, it's best to look for a freelancer who can shoot and edit it for US$1,000. If you're creating a series that will form the cornerstone of the marketing effort that will build your future success, it's best to go to an external supplier.

	Content Agency	Internal Resources	Freelancers
Pros	Quality They take the problem off your hands Security Agreed cost up front	They understand your branding/ ways of working Lower cost Usually there when you need them	Lowest price May be excellent Opportunity to direct their work/be more involved Opportunity to pick specialists for each project
Cons	High cost Onboarding challenges May leave you 'holding the baby'	May get stale Challenges with scaling Add to the company headcount May end up costing more than anticipated	Higher risk Difficult to judge their quality before working with them May be difficult to manage

Table 1. Pros and cons of different production providers

CHAPTER 14

DISTRIBUTION PLANNING

This chapter comes at this stage of the book because this is where the physical distribution bit of the process sits. In reality, *you need to be thinking about how your content is going to be distributed from the initial-briefing stage.* Because of this, you'll find that much of this chapter refers back to Chapters 6 and 7 on briefing and audience, respectively. I'd recommend reading them to help you to get the most out of this chapter.

By now, you'll have a perfectly crafted film, or series of films, which will enrapture all who see it/them. The problem is that the key part of that sentence is the last bit – 'all who see it/them'. **Having the film is important, but getting it seen is essential.** A video with no viewers is pointless, no matter how good it is. This chapter will focus on how you get the right people to see your content to drive the outcome you're after. We'll start by looking at the underpinnings of a successful content plan. We'll then look at the various different platforms available, the tools to help you and how data can help to optimise the impact of your content.

"Those who fail to plan are planning to fail."

– Benjamin Franklin

Why a content distribution plan is critical

Producing a film without a clear plan is a really great way to waste your time and money. Historically, we've made and delivered a number of films for clients who say, "I put it on my website, but how can I get it more views?" Unfortunately, this is the wrong way around to do it, as the way that it will be distributed will nearly always inform the way the film is made. Ideally, you should create your plan in unison with the creative for the production. This allows it to link up across the different platforms, which will cross promote and enhance the perception of the campaign through consistency.

"Everyone's got a plan till they get punched in the face."
– 'Iron' Mike Tyson

The plan defines your route to success, but it will often not work out exactly as you envisaged it. The most important point to having a plan is that formulating it forces you to think through the possible outcomes. In having a plan agreed, you have a baseline from which you can make shifts as you work towards success.

How to Create an Effective Content Distribution Plan

I recommend you do the following:

- ✓ Think about how this will align with your business goals
- ✓ Define success; what exactly are you trying to achieve?
- ✓ Define/review the target audience
- ✓ Audit all of your existing content
- ✓ Define the delivery method
- ✓ Write the distribution plan
- ✓ Make some amazing content
- ✓ Run the plan
- ✓ Learn, revise and rerun the plan
- ✓ Repeat the previous steps until you achieve the successful completion of your goals

Let's look at these steps in a little more detail.

Think about how this will align with your business goals/ strategy

All of the content you produce should align with your broader business objectives. Before you start your project/campaign, think about how its successful completion will help you achieve your business strategy. This could be through improving recruitment, explaining and selling more products, or launching a new office. Whatever it is, make sure it aligns with your goals. If it doesn't, is it the right thing to do? Do you need to rethink? It is a tragedy to get to the end of a time-consuming and expensive process only to realise that you didn't need to do it in the first place.

Define success; what exactly are you trying to achieve?

The first step to a successful strategy is defining exactly what you're trying to achieve; i.e. what does success look like? Are you looking to reduce staff turnover, have a successful launch of a new product or just improve awareness of your brand? The goals for any project should be tied to your broader brand strategy.

You should have a clear goal for all your marketing, specific goals for video in general, and, beyond this, each piece of video content should have specific goals it was created to achieve.

All of these objectives should be defined as SMART goals (that is, specific, measurable, achievable, realistic and time bound). So, "We want more applications" becomes "We want to increase online portal job applications by 25% over the period from 1st June to 30th September."

This then gives you a clear yardstick against which to assess your success. Did applications increase, but only by 12%? Did written applications increase instead? Did the material you shared get a lot of interest, but then fail to drive actual applications?

Beware: Make sure KPIs directly reflect the desired outcomes

Be aware that the goals that you set for your content will shape the way that your creative evolves. If you set the wrong KPIs and then aim to optimise them, it will start to skew your project away from where you want it to be. You need to be very careful that the KPIs represent exactly what you're looking to achieve. For example, if you want to improve the quality of applications for a new job role, for example, it won't necessarily be enough to simply track the overall number of applicants. If you were to set that as a goal, it might be easiest to increase the number of applicants by getting poorer-quality candidates to apply.

What can we measure?

One of the most significant challenges to face online video is that – as we covered earlier – much of the immediate benefit is intangible. Improved brand affinity, while leading to longer-term success, isn't the easiest thing to measure with a ruler. Because of this, it is essential to define a KPI that is measurable. This tends to boil down to three different types of metric, which are as follows.

1. Awareness

This is the simplest form of measurement and the easiest to record. How many people have seen the video, how far through did they watch and where were they watching from? All this information is easy to get from YouTube, Vimeo, Wistia or whichever hosting site carries the video. This is the least valuable metric because it's so superficial. You don't know who's watching, whether they hated it or whether they were even looking at the screen. Facebook counts a 'view' as any portion of the video being visible for 2 seconds or more. That's not really long enough for anything meaningful.

It's more useful for 200 of your target audience to see your content than it is for 200,000 people from the wrong group. There's also the dubious nature of the viewing figures. It's possible to boost video by buying views, usually though automated bots. While this might trick a potential viewer into thinking the video is more popular than it is, this is really no substitute for genuinely great content that people actually want to watch.

2. Engagement

This leads us on to engagement. This might include the audience liking, sharing or commenting on your videos. This is a major step up from simple views. As a very rough rule of thumb, most pieces of decent content get around one engagement for every ten views. If you're focusing on this metric, set your bar high; it's worth pushing for comments and shares, rather than likes. For many people, a 'like' is someone who wasn't moved enough by your content to want to share it.

3. Action

Action is ultimately what we're after. Making video in the business sphere is about driving actions, so it makes sense to use them as a desired metric. Actions can be almost anything, from applications for a job role to donations on a crowdfunding page. The useful thing about focusing on these as goals is that they are tangible and indisputable.

One thing that is disputable, though, is the extent to which an individual piece of content drove a specific action. If the viewer stays on the site and directly makes a purchase, for example, that's straightforward enough. Where it gets more complex is when the action isn't directly attributable to the content. The target might watch a video, go away, think about it, discuss it with a friend, and then go and make a purchase from an unconnected source. You can measure that on a very general level, but video is rarely used in isolation. It forms part of a wider communications matrix, all aspects of which are driving towards one or many different goals.

It's important to know how much impact the content of the video is having versus how or where it's served to the viewer. The right video at the wrong time may not generate the response it will at the right time. That doesn't necessarily mean that there was anything wrong with the output.

Define/review the target audience

The first step in developing your content distribution plan is understanding exactly who your audience are. Luckily, if you've been through the briefing process thoroughly, you should have gained a good understanding then. Once you have a really clear idea of the people you need to reach, you can start to think about where you might be able to reach them. As we examined in Chapter 7, it's important to understand where in the buying cycle they are, so that you can supply the right type of content at the right time. Programmatic marketing can help you with this (see box on page 229).

Audit all of your existing content

Before you begin, it's important to know exactly what you've produced in the past, so that you can learn any lessons from what worked or could have been better. It also allows you to avoid duplication, and gives you the opportunity to reuse/optimise some of the content, if appropriate. The chances are that your business will already have lots of video content that you've produced over the years. Some of it will be good, and some bad, but it's surprising what can be done in the production process to standardise the look of material from different sources. Being thrifty here allows you to put more of the budget where you'll be able to see it.

Define the delivery method

Since we started Casual, in the early days of video being online, I can count the number of films we've delivered as a hard copy on my fingers. That's out of nearly 10,000 films. Because of this, it's safe to assume that you'll be sharing your content online; it's the cheapest and most efficient way to do it. You need to think about your audience and where they are going to be able to watch your videos.

We had one client that was looking to run some internal communications videos to keep its staff up to date with what was happening in the wider company. These were power-station workers. Their average age was in the late 50s, and smartphone/computer usage was a single-digit percentage. We looked, for a time, at the possibility of cutting the films into short outputs and then having them playing on screens that we'd put up in the men's room and other communal areas where the audience would spend time. In the end, they didn't go ahead with it, but the example illustrates the creative thinking that can be employed to get the right people to see your films.

One of the really cool things about the advances in augmented reality (AR) is that we can now share video content with consumers at different points in their buying cycle. For example, if we're promoting a mustard, we may know that when a shopper is in the shop they might be interested in where the mustard is grown. If they look at the pot with their AR-enabled phone, they might be shown an interview with the farmer, the ingredients, or some footage of the farm and processing facility it was manufactured in. This might sound a little too open for comfort, but this level of transparency is coming – consumers will demand it. When they get home, the customer looks at the pot again and this time they are shown recipes, possibly defined by the other ingredients they bought, or the day of the week and their past eating habits (data protection allowing – see box on page 201).The fact is that the number of ways that you can share your content with your audience is growing by the day. Don't always think that the only place they will watch your content is YouTube or Facebook, because it's not.

There are three different avenues for distributing your content online. The content that you produce for each channel may be slightly different, in terms of the length (as we saw in Chapter 12), style and CTA.

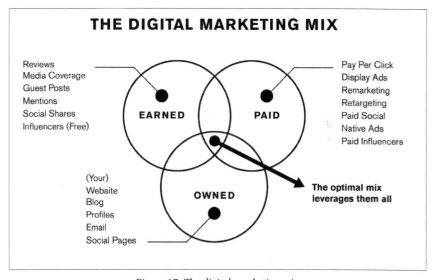

THE DIGITAL MARKETING MIX

Reviews
Media Coverage
Guest Posts
Mentions
Social Shares
Influencers (Free)

EARNED

PAID

Pay Per Click
Display Ads
Remarketing
Retargeting
Paid Social
Native Ads
Paid Influencers

(Your)
Website
Blog
Profiles
Email
Social Pages

OWNED

The optimal mix leverages them all

Figure 17. The digital marketing mix

Owned media

These are all the channels for which you own the control. They include your website, social pages, intranet and internal staff communications. The information here is what your brand says and what people say to you. Around 90% of online conversations about brands do not take place on their own pages. This means you have to get out there to influence these conversations.

Earned media

Your earned media are shares of your content, and articles and blogs written about your channels. This is what people say about you. You earn views here by creating content that people want to engage with and share.

Paid media

Your paid channels are, unsurprisingly, the ones you have to pay for. They include paid posts, traditional advertising and programmatic marketing (see the box following this cartoon).

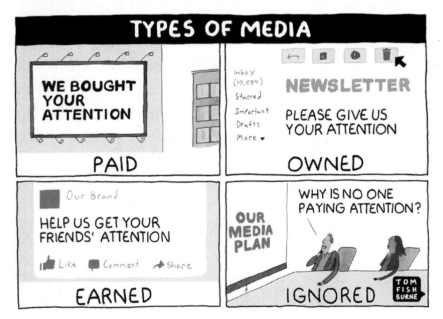

NO MATTER WHERE IT GOES, YOUR AIM IS TO MAKE CONTENT THAT PEOPLE LOVE

Programmatic Marketing

This is using software to buy advertising space in real time. This has made a process that used to take a significant amount of time almost instantaneous. This is useful to you because it allows you to accurately target your audience with your content. It's successful because it's efficient and it reduces the amount of money that gets spent on showing content to the wrong people.

The system also allows you to continually optimise the targeting, so that it improves over time. It also allows different types of content to be shown to a specific viewer, depending on which pieces of content they have watched or interacted with in the past. (See Chapter 7 on your target audience for more information on the different stages of the customer lifecycle.)

It's not perfect, though. There was a scandal in March 2017 when a number of major advertisers pulled spend from YouTube as it emerged that the platform had displayed their commercials alongside extremist content. There have also been questions around ad fraud and the amount of budget that goes on showing content to bots.

Dynamic creative optimisation

Another element of programmatic marketing is dynamic creative optimisation or DCO. This takes the same understanding of the audience that programmatic retargeting does, but uses it to serve content that is optimised to engage them. For example, there are two people who are interested in buying a car. One is a successful, single woman in her 30s, and the other is a father of three in his 40s. DCO would allow the same company to advertise directly to them both, with content that is designed to pique their interest. It could do this by serving the woman an ad for a two-seater convertible and the father an ad for a people carrier. This makes the content far more effective, and it's a step towards the full personalisation of marketing. DCO

> also allows content to be optimised for other factors such as viewing time and location, the weather, the news, etc. That is any element that might improve the effectiveness of the project.

Write the distribution plan

Now you should be ready to start writing your plan. Your plan should have the following ten elements:

1. **Project number**

   Using project numbers helps to keep track of all the different pieces of content you're creating. Each film should have its own specific number, which allows you to limit the risk of duplication/ misunderstanding.

2. **Publication date**

   These tell you when each piece of content needs to be published. Your separate production plan will include the key dates in the production.

3. **Topic**

   What is the video about? What is the subject area that this output corresponds to?

4. **A/B titles**

   What is each video/piece of content called? This will help you refer to it. If you're testing a number of different titles, you can also include them here.

5. **Content/details**

   What is each piece of content about? Who or what does it include?

6. **Keywords**

   What are the keywords for the piece of content? These will also be included in the metadata of the video. This is information that is baked into the digital file when it's exported. It may also be the information that you include in the explanation section of the video on the sharing site you use.

7. **Target personas**

As we saw in Chapter 7, you'll have a number of different personas that you're targeting. Each piece of content should have one of these in mind as the primary audience. This will help you to keep the content coherent. For this reason, it's useful to include this information here.

8. **Project leader**

You may have a team of people creating or commissioning content for your marketing efforts. This helps you keep track of who needs to get the work done.

9. **Platforms**

Where will the different outputs be going?

10. **Results**

Finally, it's useful keep track of the results that each video gets. This will help you to see trends, and to understand areas where you're weaker or stronger. The results you're tracking may differ depending on the project. Because of this, it's important to note what specific results you're recording.

Proj. No.	Publ. date	Topic	A/B Titles	Content/details	Keywords	Target persona(s)	Project leader	Platforms	Results
e.g. 3482/ABC/GRAD1	e.g. 08/10/2019	e.g. Grad Recruitment	e.g. A day in the life of an [ABC company] grad	e.g. Interview-led profile film following graduate trainee.	e.g. [ABC co.], grad jobs, technology jobs, new starters, day in the life	e.g. Tech Grad Tracy	e.g. Simon Norris, HR Marketing Manager	e.g. Recruitment microsite, Youtube, Instagram, events	e.g. 25,384 views, 2,604 likes, 865 shares, 237 applications

Figure 18. Example plan

Make some amazing content

The quality of the creative messaging in your content is essential. It makes up 8/10ths of the impact of your campaign. This is where you should invest in doing it properly. A film isn't simply a film. If all you're after is a film, then of course you can and should shoot it with your iPhone. If you're serious about using video as a tool to overcome a business challenge, then do it properly.

> The better the creative, the less work you'll have to do to help it get traction, which will ultimately save you money.

Short-form content

One of the big shifts we've seen at Casual over the last few years is the growth of content atomisation. That is, taking what would have been a single output of 3 minutes or so 5 years ago, and cutting it into many different outputs to provide assets to share across the breadth of online platforms. This is how a typical atomised delivery might look (see Chapter 12 for more information on video lengths).

1 x 90-second hero film

This is the main edit of all the profile films. We call this the 'hero' because it's the main piece of content that leads the others.

3 x 90-second profile films

In this instance, these films are based on interviews with people chosen to tell the story. They are literally profiles of these individuals.

6 x 45-second social cuts for Facebook/LinkedIn

6 x 15-second social cuts for Instagram/Twitter

These social cuts each focus on slightly different elements of each story. Because you have multiple outputs, it allows you to track which ones resonate with your target audience in order to optimise the content and how you approach them in the future.

12 x banners

These are clickable banners based on the campaign. There are three for each video; once again, these are to allow for optimisation to the desired audience.

Still images

Finally, to maximise on the investment of getting everyone together for the shoot, the crew will shoot some stills, which can be used to promote the project or used wherever else they are required.

Why does this matter?

The point of creating a large number of outputs like this is that it allows you to cross promote, and use them all to create a virtuous cycle. Given how disparate your audience can be, it allows you to seed multiple pieces of content, which improves the odds of them being seen. It also helps you to maximise your return on investment in the process by getting more mileage out of the more expensive elements in the process, such as shoot days.

Going Viral

Content going viral is regarded by many as the Holy Grail of online marketing. The idea that you could create a piece of promotional content that will capture just the right combination of *je ne sais quoi* to be shared hundreds of thousands, or even millions, of times with minimal spend. It's a compelling idea, which is probably why it has held such sway. We've been asked countless times for videos to 'be viral' or to 'go viral'. That's not to say that there aren't examples of incredible success in this area, but they tend to be more through an unreliable accident, or careful planning and significant investment.

There are different levels of 'virality'. While millions or billions of views might be good for the ego, you may only need a few thousand of the right people to see it to get the result you're after. You'll be better placed to create these campaigns if you understand the psychology behind what makes people want to share them. There are a number of reasons for this, each one driven by a small dopamine release in the brain. The larger the release, the more chance that the audience will share the content. Videos that drive this amuse, surprise, endear, shock, excite, disgust or trigger nostalgia.

Beyond this, people share content for the following reasons:

» To connect over a shared interest

» To help others with products and/or relevant advice

» To boost their reputation

» To look on trend/*au fait* with the latest events

» To be involved in current trends/events

» To make a statement about themselves

» To be able to socialise offline

» To promote a cause they believe in or want to be seen to believe in

» To demonstrate their own knowledge or ability

» To start an online conversation

Having understood some of the psychology, there are a couple of extra things that will help:

Make the production extra 'tight'

To stand the best chance, you need to get rid of as much flab from the production as possible. Give the script, edit and sound design an extra pass through to make sure that only the most essential elements are there. People get bored easily. If you're going for barnstorming success (which you are), you don't want any filler in there.

Make the name/thumbnail image perfect

First impressions count. The first thing your audience will see is the title and thumbnail, so they are almost more important than the content itself. Naturally, they need to be eye-catching, but how do you get them just right?

1. **It should be impactful/match what people are searching for.** For example, 'How to Change a Road Bike Tyre' or 'Change Bike Tyres Like a Pro' is going to get a lot more hits than 'tyre_video_ final_ v.5'. This

raises another point. The title that you've been using in production should be changed before you share the video. It looks really sloppy, and isn't searchable or clickable.

2. **The name must reflect the content of the film.** If your audience can't find it because the name is too obscure, or if they do watch it but find that the title has misled them, they will let you and other users know about it. You don't want to get a load of negative reviews because your audience feel like you've duped them.

3. **A/B testing.** Just as you can optimise the content of your videos, so you must optimise the title and thumbnail. You must see which combination is the most effective at engaging your target audience. A/B testing entails sharing two or more different concepts/titles/images, and then judging which is the most effective. You do this by reviewing the responses you get from your chosen audience. For example, you may find that when you use the title, 'Top 5 Ways to Target the Tech-Savvy Grads with Video' you get a better response than when you use 'Recruiting Tech Grads – A Guide to Video'.

By focusing on the approach that gets the best response, you can continually improve the responses to your marketing. Record what works and use it to inform your future content.

Put budget behind it to get the ball rolling

Of course, if you incorporate all of this thinking, you'll be on your way to creating 'sticky' videos (i.e. ones that will stick in the mind) that people want to share. Unfortunately, despite their shining brilliance, the chance of them being plucked from obscurity and becoming overnight successes are still extremely slim without giving them a (significant) financial push. Even the best content needs to be helped to get in front of the right people. You then need to make sure that it has just the right elements that will mean they will take it, share it and enable it to grow from there.

Why you should never call it a 'final' version

Another point you may already be aware of is never call an output 'final', 'finished', 'last output', etc. I'm not particularly superstitious, but I know that there is a powerful natural force that strikes down such hubris with previously unseen, time-consuming errors. In the thousands of films we've made, and the tens of thousands of different edits that have been output, I'm not aware of a single initial 'final' version that ended up being that.

Going Live

One of the really exciting developments of recent years is the accessibility of live-video broadcasting. YouTube, Facebook Live, Snap Live Stories and Periscope have put the ability to broadcast live in the hands of consumers and brands. As with traditional TV in the past, live online broadcasts give the audience an opportunity to take part in an event, as opposed to just watching the video outputs. This has been used to great effect by many marketers.

When Chevrolet wanted to promote the launch of its 2017 Bolt EV, it used Facebook Live to share a stream from the Consumer Electronics Show of 2016. In the stream, the Chevrolet spokesperson talks about how the world of the future will significantly increase demand for electric cars. By using Facebook Live, the company was able to add to the Bolt's brand positioning by working with a platform that was considered to be new and cool by the audience. This is a good example of the old marketing adage: the medium is the message.

Events like this provide a condensation point for fans and potential buyers of the product. Once the broadcast is finished, it stays online, allowing those who missed it to access and comment on it in their own time. The engagement rates are higher too. People spend three times longer watching Facebook Live than they do watching other pre-recorded videos on the platform.

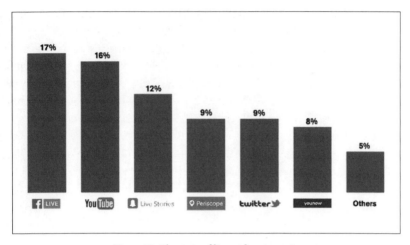

*Figure 19. The state of live-video streaming
(% of respondents who streamed live video on these platforms).*

Another great asset of live videos is that the audience find them more trustworthy than edited video. This is because they feel less overtly controlled. This makes them excellent for recruitment and employer branding, as they allow the candidate to feel like they have met members of your staff and experienced some of the company culture.

Run the plan

3, 2, 1, *go!*

Learn, revise and rerun the plan

*"That which is measured improves. That which is measured and
reported on improves exponentially."*

– Karl Pearson

All of the available data is extremely useful for evolving your video strategy (see Chapter 11 on data). It's unlikely that even the best plan will go ahead without some degree of evolution once you start working through it. The information that you can get from these platforms allows you to make small tweaks to the types of film you commission, and potentially to re-edit work that is seeing a significant drop-off at a certain point. Karl Pearson's quotation is useful because it shows the importance of taking accountability for the decisions we've taken and outcomes that result. You're more likely to learn from the pieces of content that didn't go so well than you are to learn from the ones that slightly missed the mark. Interrogate these. What was it that led to them not being so successful? Was it the time that you shared it? According to its editorial team, if men's magazine *GQ* shares a piece on 'How to create the perfect Tinder profile' on a Monday morning, it bombs. If it shares exactly the same piece on a Sunday evening, it breaks all its engagement records.[1] Presumably, young men who haven't had a successful weekend are thinking about what they can do differently on Sunday, but grafting hard on Monday morning. By testing what makes pieces work, you can begin to maximise on the effectiveness of your output, but only if you work to understand and learn from the failures.

For example, you operate a flour mill and want to promote your wares through video. You have a series of films that explain how to bake different breads that incorporate your brand of flour. By looking at the metrics from your hosting platform, it turns out that the most popular video by far is the one that explains how to bake sourdough.

You could take a few things from this: your audience is particularly interested in sourdough, the labelling of the other videos isn't as strong as the sourdough video or the films themselves aren't as strong. I'll come on to these other elements shortly, but, for now, all things being equal, you can deduce that your audience are interested in sourdough, so you can build further content that will engage them – sourdough pizza crusts, rye sourdough loaves, how to make a starter, etc. – your hipster audience won't know what's hit them.

Beyond this, you can look at whether there are particular points where the audience drop off. This could tell you one of a number of things: the video is losing pace (it got boring), it shared all the information that someone who clicked on that title was after or the title has mis-sold the content. Armed with this information, you can look at what can be done to remedy this. Through this process of incremental content evolution, you can create a journey for your audience, and continually improve the quality of your content and its relevance to the audience.

Another benefit of the analytical data is that it will show you the different demographics and geographical spread of your audience. This then allows you to tailor different content strands to the tastes of the different audiences. There is more information on how to do this properly in Chapter 7.

One of the most valuable assets for those sharing video online is that it allows for continual iterative improvement; i.e. you can publish a number of different potential angles on the same story/brief and then see which ones resonate most effectively with your audience. This means that you can learn from misses and build on successes, continually improving the effectiveness of your material with the target audience.

The various measurement analytics that you have access to are essential for this. The great thing here is that they can be really granular in helping you to work out who's watching your content, where they are and how engaged they are. Because the production of different re-edits or even different videos is now relatively cheap (compared to the distribution budget for them), it's a really efficient way to maximise the campaign's efficiency.

This can be seen in action where it was used by Sony Pictures to promote *The Greatest Showman* film. It produced a number of different adverts, each focusing on different areas of the film, characters and subplots. It found that a certain area resonated. It stopped showing the executions that weren't working, and it focused its budget on promoting the content that was working. This meant that it was able to make its marketing budget go far further and be more effective.

Repeat the previous steps until you achieve the successful completion of your goals

Errr... that title was maybe overly descriptive, but you get the picture. Keep running, learning, refining and rerunning until you achieve your goals.

In Summary: Distribution Planning

Having a coherent plan is essential for being successful with your content. You need to think about this from the outset of the project, as it will help all the content that you produce to pull in the same direction. There is a ten-step process to follow to help you succeed:

4. **All of your planning and goals should be based on your business strategy.**

5. **Define success.** What exactly are you trying to achieve? There are three main areas that we can measure: *awareness* (views), *engagement* (likes, shares and comments) and *action* (which the audience has taken as a result).

6. **Understand who and where your target audience are.** Review Chapter 7 for more information on this.

7. **Audit all of your existing content.** What have you already got and what can be reused? How can you complement it?

8. **Define the delivery method.** How are you getting the content out there? You have three main channels: owned (your website/social pages/intranet), earned (social media shares/blogs written about you) and paid (adverts/space you've paid for).

9. **Write the plan.**

10. **Make some amazing content.** The better the content, the further your budget will go.

11. **Run the plan.** *Go!*

12. **Learn, revise and rerun the plan.** Iterative improvement is essential to maximising benefits online.

13. **Repeat step 9** until you achieve the successful completion of your goals.

Some of the other things covered in this chapter are as follows.

Atomised content

Single-output brand films cost a lot and may be missed by the desired audience on social media. Because of this, we now tend to 'atomise' the same content – chopping a single film into as many as 50 different outputs, with each optimised for the platform it will be shared on.

Going viral

The idea that a piece of your content will go viral is a compelling one. In reality, to get this kind of traction you need a great idea that is well executed, and be prepared to spend a lot to seed it and get it going.

ALL NEW TECHNOLOGY CARRIES AN ELEMENT OF RISK

Going live

Live video is a great way to build a sense of occasion for your audience. It becomes a gathering point that they can be involved in while it is running, and provides content that you can then recut and share after the event. Live video is growing in popularity as more platforms offer it.

In the next and final chapter, we'll look at the ten things you need to do to make better, more-effective videos.

CHAPTER 15

THE TEN COMMANDMENTS FOR CREATING BETTER VIDEO

1. Begin with the End in Mind – What Exactly Are You Trying to Achieve?

The best way to get somewhere is to know that you're trying to get there from the outset. Almost every project that doesn't come out well can be traced back to the initial briefing. Be really clear, and make sure all the stakeholders are aligned and know what the project is aiming for (see *What Are You Trying to Achieve*, pages 133-5).

2. Know the Audience

Having a clear understanding of exactly who the audience are is essential to making content that resonates with them. The better you know them, the better and more effective the content that you'll be able to produce for them. This partially explains why YouTube video bloggers have been so successful (see Youtubers, pages 58-60).

3. Create a Briefing Document

Getting alignment across all of the people involved in the project is key to its success. It can often feel like you don't really need a briefing document, but it's always required. If it's worth making a film about, it's worth taking a few minutes to jot down who it's for and why you're doing it. Even if this is just in note form (see Chapter 6).

4. Make It Shorter

Nearly every film ever made could benefit from losing 10–20% or more of its length. Condensing the, no doubt, killer content that you have will only improve its average quality, making the film more energetic, more impactful and just generally better. This can take real discipline, but it's always worth it (see Chapter 12).

IT'S IMPORTANT TO BE REALLY CLEAR ABOUT OBJECTIVES

5. Be Bold

Your content will have to compete with so much noise, so you need to give it every possible chance to succeed. This means being bold with your thinking, being bold with your creative ideas and being bold with your strategy. Don't produce work that doesn't aim to be great. It's not worth it.

6. Think About Distribution from the Outset

Making sure that your film gets seen is essential. Where it's going to be shared plays an important part in the way that it'll be made: the style of the messaging, the length and the CTA. Because of this, it's important that the distribution of your project is thought about from the initial-briefing meeting. This will ensure the whole project is consistent, and it will improve your return on investment (see Chapter 14).

7. Be Consistent

Getting the results you're after takes time and perseverance. It's unlikely that you'll see results overnight. Because of this, you need to agree on a plan and then see it through. This will require consistency. Most YouTube stars spent years broadcasting to a handful of subscribers before their audiences grew to the millions some of them enjoy today. What sets the successes apart is their ability to keep going. You should also keep reiterating your content as you build on successes and learn from setbacks. Understand what it is about the successful content that resonates with your audience. Do more of this to continually make your material better and more fit for purpose.

8. Make the Most of What You Have

Filmmaking is a creative process. Because of this, it can flex to incorporate all sorts of things that you might want it to. Whether you already have lots of great footage, a stunning office or some stunningly talented staff, you should include this in the briefing document, so that the creative team can make the most of it in their thinking.

9. Do it Properly: Don't be Wasteful, but Don't be Cheap

Video is an extremely flexible medium, and technology gets cheaper and more accessible by the day. Because of this, it's amazing what can be achieved with even a limited budget, particularly if you're able to do a lot of the production work yourself. Don't be cheap, though. To achieve great results, you have to invest in doing it properly. More budget means more time, and more time means better thinking, which will lead to a better result (see Chapter 8).

10. Enjoy It

Last, but not least, it's essential that you enjoy the process. Of course, it can be challenging and sometimes frustrating, but the very best films that we make as a company are with the clients who enjoy the process. They are open minded and want to work with us to make it good. If you open your mind to the possibility that this can be an enriching, exciting and fulfilling experience, then great work will follow.

CONCLUSION

I hope that the information in this book will allow you to capitalise on the opportunities that video offers. You are the commissioner of an exciting new technology, which is only coming of age right now. We're living through a shift from broadcasting to narrowcasting. This means that you can use video to directly communicate with small sections of your target audience, and build relationships of a kind that were impossible just a handful of years ago. I hope that this book has given you the tools you need to get even more out of this technology.

The medium continues to evolve by the day. Virtual Reality, Augmented Reality and interactive video are burgeoning technologies. All of which allow you to craft a richer and more dynamically involving experience for your audience. This will facilitate earning their loyalty and affinity in stimulating, resilient and profitable new ways. This capability is at your fingertips right now. Many businesses are grasping it. There are hundreds of excellent agencies and companies out there that can help you to harness them. Do this, and you'll be ahead of the curve and on your way into the exciting future of broadcasting.

With this in mind, there are three main points that I'd like you to take from this book:

1. Technology has democratised the power of video.

2. You need to think about the video you share as an additional product.

3. Your business's purpose and values should be your cornerstone.

1. Technology has democratised the power of video

Video is the most effective way to generate emotion in an online audience. In the hands of a storyteller, it makes facts memorable, ideas shareable and the intangible tangible. It gives you the power to reach past your audience's increasingly distracted heads and into their hearts. Your audience are more video savvy than ever. Video makes up 80% of online traffic – it's the preferred means of communication online, whether your audience are senior executives or school children.

The technology to create and distribute quality video is in all of our pockets. The smartphones that are in the hands of consumers can shoot, edit and share video. We now have access to what was the production capability of a multi-million-dollar TV studio only a handful of years ago. Having a thorough understanding of the tools and medium is essential.

The pace of change means that many of the senior executives who now oversee these functions and lead these businesses don't understand the capability available to the businesses they oversee. Your businesses and all of us, whether we like it or not, are the owners of a content channel. You need to use this capability to create content that engages, entertains, educates and informs your stakeholders – your audience. To fail to do this is to fall behind in an area that offers relatively simple and cost-effective wins. Improving perceived value is far easier and cheaper than improving the physical value of your products and services.

Whatever you're looking to achieve, look for great stories around your brand and business, and tell them with this brilliant, easily accessible tool. An engaging story about your producers can completely change your customers' perception of your products, and a story of staff solidarity can retain your workforce and drive recruitment. This isn't necessarily about spending larger sums, it's about being completely clear regarding your objectives and your audience, and then creating a coherent content plan that accomplishes the former by resonating with the latter.

2. You need to think about the video you share as an additional product

Effective content should build the perceived value of your brand. As we've seen, it's impossible to distinguish between perceived and actual value in the buyer's eyes. Because of this, it's useful to think about your content as an additional product that your business produces. Done properly, it really is that important and useful. Whatever you're trying to achieve, if the stories you share are genuine, video gives you the opportunity to build a strong and lasting affinity with your audience. This is an affinity that will show on your balance sheet through stronger customer loyalty, better sales and better staff retention.

The best way to do this is to create content that is of value to your audience. There are a number of different ways to think about how to do this, but I like the idea that your content should be TRUE to them; that is, timely, relevant, useful and/or entertaining. Again, audience understanding is key to this. You need to know exactly whom you're communicating with so that you can be perfectly 'on their level'. A failure here can actively damage your brand in the eyes of the consumer. No one wants to do the brand equivalent of dad dancing.

It being an additional product means that you need to take your content and its potential seriously. The world is watching. Your employees are your customers; your internal brand is your external brand. Corporate video is no longer about poor-quality tapes shared with a groaning/smirking captive audience. It has encroached on your external marketing and become brand video. No matter what the video is produced for – sales, training, recruitment or a how-to – it'll become part of your audience's perception of your brand. It needs to be considered, it needs to be appropriate and it needs to be right. Poor content can damage your brand in the same way that a product problem can.

3. Your business's purpose and values should be your cornerstone

The best way to keep your content consistent is to ground it in your business purpose. Having a clearly defined purpose, or a 'Why?', as a business carries a wide range of benefits, including more-engaged staff, better differentiation in the marketplace and better recruitment. A clearly defined and communicated purpose acts like a North Star for your business operations. It helps all of your stakeholders to understand where they stand, which allows them to decide whether or not your values align with theirs. While there may be some who will exclude themselves, the engagement and loyalty of those who remain will more than make up for it. Having a clear purpose is about defining what makes your business special and about defining what the difference you make in the world is.

Purpose is a really useful resource for your content because it allows you to show that you care at the same time as providing consistency. Not that all of your content needs to be directly about it, but you should be able to draw a direct line to it. For example, BMW's purpose is 'The joy of driving', so films about car maintenance work, but films about ice cream won't. That example might seem a little flippant, but, as an exercise, you should find it more instructive than it might at first appear. Do holidays work? Yes if you can enjoy driving on/to them, but no if you can't.

If you choose to make and share films about the good causes that you're involved in, which is an excellent place to look for ideas, make sure you're walking the walk and not just talking the talk. Action is essential, or you'll be eaten alive online. You have to be genuine and do the things that you say you do. Just as the fire of video can provide life, sustenance and warmth, so it can badly burn or even kill you. Don't make the mistake of using unsubstantiated spin.

We're living at an extremely exciting time. Technological advancement means that, as a planet, we're living longer, more prosperously and more peacefully than ever before – despite what you might think. There are, of course, great challenges that we need to draw together to overcome. We've never been in a better position to do this than we are now. Don't be cynical. Use the available tools to take action.

Be Bold

Finally, if your mind is marooned on a desert island and you can only save one point from this book before your brain sinks beneath the waves, make it this: **Be bold.**

Everyone wants to be Apple,
but no one wants to be Steve Jobs

You have an amazing tool in your armoury. A tool that, after over a century, is finally coming of age. But you must be brave, and you have to be bold to really make the most of it. Try the more challenging creative route. Take the less trodden path. Take calculated risks – nothing is final bar death (and you've really messed up if your creative kills you). You can build on and learn from outcomes that aren't exactly as you hoped they would be. Aim for excellence in everything you do. Just go for it. It will pay you back many, many times over.

Next Steps:

"Knowledge without action is futile."
– Abu Bakr, AD 573 to 634

I hope that this book has opened your eyes to the power of video for your business. By now I'm sure you're straining to get started. Here are a number of different paths you might want to take from here:

1. Book a content strategy consultation or a presentation of any of the ideas in this book, visit: www.newfirebook.com

2. Contact me on LinkedIn, let me your thoughts on the book or where you're at in your content journey: www.linkedin.com/in/nickfrancisfilm/

3. Take a moment to review this book on Amazon – you'll help other people to find it.

4. Get to know Casual better by booking a "Lunch and Learn" – the latest films, ideas and techniques, presented to your team, and they bring lunch. Contact: hello@casualfilms.com

5. Continue the learnings in this book, subscribe to the Make Video Work for Business blog: www.casualfilms.com/blog

If you would like to order multiple copies for your team please get in touch via the newfirebook.com website. There are considerable discounts for bulk orders. I am also open to tailoring copies to your requirements with specific information.

The Casual Films Academy

A proportion of the profits from this book will go to the Casual Academy charity. The Academy trains young people in video production, by getting them to make films for local charities that would not be able to afford them otherwise. This creates a double win: the young people get the experience and training from the course, along with a film for their showreel; and the charity gets a nearly free film that it can use for its promotions.

Set up in 2012, it has trained over 120 people in various skills, including pitching, scriptwriting, producing, shooting and editing. The plan for the charity is to create an app, which will guide filmmakers around the world through the process of running one of these courses. If you think you can help, if you know anyone who might like to get involved, or if you'd like to make a donation, please get in touch. Visit www.thecasualacademy.com for more information.

If you would like to order multiple copies for your team then get in touch via the newfirebook.com website. There are considerable discounts for even relatively small bulk orders.

REFERENCES

Preface & Introduction

1. Polly W. Wiessner, *Embers of Society: Firelight Talk among the Ju/'hoansi Bushmen* (National Academy of Sciences, 30th September 2014).

2. Statista, "Number of Smartphone Users Worldwide from 2014 to 2020 (in Billions)", Statista, 2018. Accessed on: 6th September 2018. https://www.statista.com/statistics/330695/number-of-smartphone-users-worldwide/

3. Cisco, *Cisco Visual Networking Index: Forecast and Methodology, 2016–2021* (Cisco, 2017).

4. Interview with Vice Media Founder Shane Smith, Cannes Lions International Festival of Creativity, Cannes, June 2016.

5. Simon Sinek, *Start with Why* (Penguin Random House, 2011).

6. Matthew Syed, *Black Box Thinking* (Hodder and Stoughton, 2015).

7. Rory Sutherland, Interview with the Author, London, October 2017.

Chapter 1

1. Cisco, *Cisco Visual Networking Index: Forecast and Methodology, 2016–2021* (Cisco, 2017).

2. John Yorke, *Into the Woods: How Stories Work and Why We Tell Them* (Penguin, 2013).

3. Jonah Sachs, *Winning the Story Wars: Why Those Who Tell – and Live – the Best Stories Will Rule the Future* (Boston, MA: Harvard Business Review Press, 2012).

4. *Oxford Dictionaries*, s.v. "empathy", accessed 6th September 2018, https://en.oxforddictionaries.com/definition/empathy

5. Professor Talma Hendler and Dr Gal Raz, *Forking Cinematic Paths to the Self: Neurocinematically Informed Model of Empathy in Motion Pictures* (School of Psychological Sciences, Tel Aviv University, 2014).

6. IKEA, "*The Lamp*", directed by Spike Jonze (Crispin Porter + Bogusky, 2002).

Chapter 2

1. Institute of Practitioners in Advertising, *IPA Touchpoints Wave 2. September 2007 – February 2008* (London, UK: IPA, 2008).

2. Institute of Practitioners in Advertising, *IPA Touchpoints Wave 6 April 2016* (London, UK: IPA, 2016).

3. Phil Shaw, *"10 Rules for TV Strategy"* (Ipsos ASI, London, December 2014).

4. Google Dynamic Logic effectiveness study, quoted in "Online Ads Not Working for You? Blame the Creative", AdAge, 20th October 2009. Accessed on: 15th December 2017. http://adage.com/article/digital/digital-online-ads-working-blame-creative/139795/

5. Tom Peters and Robert Waterman Jr., *In Search of Excellence* (Harper Business Essentials, 1982).

6. Ludwig von Mises, 1933, *Epistemological Problems of Economics*, Third Edition, Translated by: George Reisman (D Van Nostrand Co., 1960).

Chapter 3

1. Content Marketing Institute, "B2B Content Marketing: 2017 Benchmarks, Budgets, and Trends-North America", Content Marketing Institute, 2017. Accessed on: 23rd February 2018. https://contentmarketinginstitute.com/wp-content/uploads/2016/09/2017_B2B_Research_FINAL.pdf

2. PageFair, The State of the Blocked Web: 2017 Global Adblock Report (Page Fair, 2017).

3. Juniper Research, *Worldwide Digital Advertising: 2016–2020* (London, UK: Juniper Research, 2016).

4. PageFair, *The State of the Blocked Web: 2017 Global Adblock Report* (Page Fair, 2017).

5. Seth Godin, *Permission Marketing: Turning Strangers into Friends and Friends into Customers* (Simon & Schuster, 1999).

6. Jason Miller, "How to Build an Owned Media Empire", presentation, 2016 B2B MarketingProfs Forum. Accessed on: 4th June 2018. https://www.slideshare.net/LImarketingsolutions/how-to-build-an-owned-media-empire

7. Think with Google, "Build a content plan", Google, October 2015. Accessed on: 3rd May 2018. https://www.thinkwithgoogle.com/marketing-resources/youtube/build-a-content-plan/

8. Dave Lloyd, "SEO for Success in Video Marketing", Adobe Blog, 20th April 2015. Accessed on: 4th June 2018. https://theblog.adobe.com/seo-for-success-in-video-marketing/

9. Animoto, *The Animoto Online and Social Video Marketing Study 2015* (New York, NY: Animoto, 2015).

10. Ibid.

11. Les Binet and Peter Field, *Media in Focus – Marketing Effectiveness in the Digital Era* (London, UK: Institute for Practitioners in Advertising, 2017).

12. Jason Miller, "The Story Behind The Big Rock", EMEA Blog, 8th February 2018. Accessed on: 9th June 2018. https://business.linkedin.com/en-uk/marketing-solutions/blog/posts/content-marketing/2018/The-story-behind-The-Big-Rock

13. Ibid.

14. Les Binet and Peter Field, *Media in Focus – Marketing Effectiveness in the Digital Era* (London, UK: Institute for Practitioners in Advertising, 2017).

15. Ibid.

Chapter 4

1. Edelman, *2018 Edelman Global Trust Barometer Survey* (Chicago, IL: Edelman, 2018).

2. Don Tapscott and David Ticoll, *The Naked Corporation: How the Age of Transparency Will Revolutionize Business* (New York, NY: Free Press, 2012).

3. Edelman, *2018 Edelman Global Trust Barometer Survey* (Chicago, IL: Edelman, 2018).

4. Unilever, "Unilever's Sustainable Living Plan Continues to Fuel Growth", Unilever, 10th May 2018. Accessed on: 23rd June 2018. https://www.unilever.com/news/press-releases/2018/unilevers-sustainable-living-plan-continues-to-fuel-growth.html

5. Oxford Dictionaries, s.v. "purpose", accessed 6th September 2018. https://en.oxforddictionaries.com/definition/purpose

6. Bill Damon, *Path to Purpose: How Young People Find Their Calling in Life* (Simon & Schuster, 2009).

7. Simon Sinek, *Start with Why* (Penguin Random House, 2011).

8. US Department of Labor, "Number of Jobs, Labor Market Experience, And Earnings Growth Among Americans at 50: Results from a Longitudinal Survey", Bureau of Labor Statistics, 2017. Accessed on: 3rd April 2018. https://www.bls.gov/news.release/pdf/nlsoy.pdf.

9. Deloitte, "Deloitte Global Millennial Survey 2017: Apprehensive Millennials: Seeking stability and opportunities in an uncertain world", Deloitte, 2017. Accessed on: 2nd April 2018. https://www2.deloitte.com/content/dam/Deloitte/global/Documents/About-Deloitte/gx-deloitte-millennial-survey-2017-executive-summary.pdf

10. Ibid.

11. Cone Communications, "Social Impact Study: The Next Cause Evolution", Cone Communications. Accessed on: 24th May 2018. http://www.conecomm.com/research-blog/2017-csr-study

12. Nielsen, "The Sustainability Imperative: New Insights on Consumer Expectations", Nielsen, 2015. Accessed on: 24th May 2018. http://www.nielsen.com/content/dam/corporate/us/en/reports-downloads/2015-reports/global-sustainability-report-oct-2015.pdf

13. Unilever, "Our Vision", Unilever. Accessed on: 23rd June 2018. https://www.unilever.com/about/who-we-are/our-vision/

14. Emma Featherstone, "British Fashion Chain Jigsaw Celebrates Immigration in New Campaign", *The Independent*, London, 13th October 2017. Accessed on: 23rd February 2018. https://www.independent.co.uk/news/business/news/jigsaw-immigration-new-campaign-celebration-british-values-style-high-street-fashion-brand-a7999256.html

15. Thomas Hobbs, "Jigsaw's 'Love Immigration' wins Marketing Week Readers' Campaign of the Year", *Marketing Week*, 22nd December 2017. Accessed on: 10th September 2018. https://www.marketingweek.com/2017/12/22/jigsaw-wins-readers-campaign-of-the-year/?nocache=true&login_errors%5B0%5D=invalidcombo&_lsnonce=6f1ec40dd1&rememberme=1

16. Cone Communications, "Social Impact Study: The Next Cause Evolution", Cone Communications, 2013. Accessed on: 24th May 2018. http://www.conecomm.com/research-blog/2017-csr-study

17. Kim Coupounas, Raphael Bemporad and Laura Palmeiro, "How the B Corp Movement Intersects with Global Brands", presentation, 12th September 2017. Accessed on: 23rd February 2018. https://s3.amazonaws.com/sbweb/slideshow/B+Corp+Danone+BBMG+SB+Webinar_master+slides+(1).pdf

18. World Bank Group, "Ending Extreme Poverty and Sharing Prosperity: Progress and Policies", World Bank Group, 2015. Accessed on: 24th February 2018. http://pubdocs.worldbank.org/en/109701443800596288/PRN03Oct2015TwinGoals.pdf

19. John Kerry, "Address at the University of Virginia - Investing in a Strong Foreign Policy", US Department of State Website, 20th February 2013. Accessed on: 24th February 2018. https://2009-2017.state.gov/secretary/remarks/2013/02/205021.htm

20. Thomas L. Friedman, *Thank You for Being Late: An Optimist's Guide to Thriving in the age of Accelerations* (New York, NY: Farrar, Straus and Giroux, 2016).

21. Anna Levesque, "Why 'Keep Your Paddle in the Water' is Bad Advice for Beginners", Mind Body Paddle, July 2014. Accessed on: 3rd March 2018. https://mindbodypaddle.com/5829/keep-paddle-water-bad-advice-beginners/

22. Thomas L. Friedman, *Thank You for Being Late: An Optimist's Guide to Thriving in the Age of Accelerations* (New York, NY: Farrar, Straus and Giroux, 2016).

23. The Business and Sustainable Development Commission, "Better Business, Better World Report", The Business and Sustainable Development Commission, 2017. Accessed on: May 3rd 2018, http://report.businesscommission.org

24. Peter F. Drucker, *Managing in a Time of Great Change* (Boston, MA: Dutton, 1995), p. 84.

25. McKinsey Global Institute, "Measuring the Economic Impact of Short-Termism", McKinsey, February 2017. Accessed on: 3rd March 2018. https://www.mckinsey.com/~/media/mckinsey/global%20themes/long%20term%20capitalism/where%20companies%20with%20a%20long%20term%20view%20outperform%20their%20peers/measuring-the-economic-impact-of-short-termism.ashx

26. Dominic Barton, Jonathan Bailey and Joshua Zoffer, "Rising to the Challenge of Short-termism", FCLT Global, September 2016. Accessed on: 5th March 2018. https://www.fcltglobal.org/docs/default-source/default-document-library/fclt-global-rising-to-the-challenge.pdf

27. Larry Fink, "Annual Letter to CEOs, 2018 - A Sense of Purpose", BlackRock. Accessed on: 3rd March 2018. https://www.blackrock.com/corporate/en-us/investor-relations/larry-fink-ceo-letter

28. Jennifer Riel and Roger L. Martin, *Creating Great Choices: A Leader's Guide to Integrative Thinking* (Boston, MA: Harvard Business Review Press, 2017).

29. Unilever, "The Unilever Sustainable Living Plan", Unilever.com. Accessed on: 10th March 2018. https://www.unilever.com/sustainable-living/

30. Unilever, "Unilever's Sustainable Living Plan Continues to Fuel Growth", Unilever. com. Accessed on: 10th March 2018. https://www.unilever.com/news/press-releases/2018/unilevers-sustainable-living-plan-continues-to-fuel-growth.html

31. Cone Communications, "Social Impact Study: The Next Cause Evolution", Cone Communications, 2013. Accessed on: 24th May 2018. http://www.conecomm.com/research-blog/2017-csr-study

32. Ibid.

33. Oxford Dictionaries, s.v. "greenwash", accessed 6th September 2018, https://en.oxforddictionaries.com/definition/greenwash

34. Eric L. Lane, "Greenwashing 2.0", *Columbia Journal of Environmental Law*, Vol. 38, No. 2. (2013).

35. CorpWatch, "Greenwash Factsheet", CorpWatch, 2001. Accessed on: 23rd June 2018. http://www.corpwatch.org/article/greenwash-fact-sheet

36. Ibid.

37. EcoWatch, "America's Deadly Love Affair with Bottled Water Has to End", EcoWatch. com, 24th September 2015. Accessed on: 24th March 2018. https://www.ecowatch.com/americas-deadly-love-affair-with-bottled-water-has-to-end-1882099598.html

38. Nielsen, "The Sustainability Imperative: New Insights on Consumer Expectations October 2015", Nielsen. Accessed on: 31st March 2018. http://www.nielsen.com/content/dam/corporate/us/en/reports-downloads/2015-reports/global-sustainability-report-oct-2015.pdf

Chapter 6

1. Steven Covey, *The Seven Habits of Highly Effective People: Powerful Lessons in Personal Change* (Simon & Schuster, 2013).

Chapter 7

1. David Carr, "Giving Viewers What They Want", *The New York Times*, 24th February 2013. Accessed on: 20th February 2018. https://www.nytimes.com/2013/02/25/business/media/for-house-of-cards-using-big-data-to-guarantee-its-popularity.html

2. Oxford Dictionaries, s.v. "psychographics", accessed 6th September 2018, https://en.oxforddictionaries.com/definition/psychographics

3. Dusty DiMercurio, "The Marketing Funnel Is Dead: Rethinking Content and the Customer Experience", presentation, ThinkContent, New York, June 2018.

Chapter 8

1. Phil Shaw, "10 Rules for TV Strategy" (Ipsos ASI, London, December 2014).

2. Google Dynamic Logic effectiveness study quoted in "Online Ads Not Working for You? Blame the Creative", AdAge.com, 20th October 2009. Accessed on: 15th December 2017. http://adage.com/article/digital/digital-online-ads-working-blame-creative/139795/

Chapter 9

1. James Hurman, *The Case for Creativity: Three Decades Evidence of the Link Between Imaginative Marketing and Commercial Success* (London, UK: Cannes Lions Publishing, 2016).

2. Phil Shaw, "10 Rules for TV Strategy" (London, UK: Ipsos ASI, December 2014).

3. Google Dynamic Logic effectiveness study quoted in "Online Ads Not Working for You? Blame the Creative." AdAge.com, 20th October 2009. Accessed on: 15th December 2017. http://adage.com/article/digital/digital-online-ads-working-blame-creative/139795/

4. James Webb Young, *A Technique for Producing Ideas* (Seattle, WA: Stellar Editions, 2016).

5. Hal Gregersen, "Better Brainstorming", Harvard Business Review, March – April 2018.

6. Google Dynamic Logic effectiveness study quoted in "Online Ads Not Working for You? Blame the Creative." AdAge.com, 20th October 2009. Accessed on: 15th December 2017. http://adage.com/article/digital/digital-online-ads-working-blame-creative/139795/

Chapter 11

1. Ken Auletta, *Frenemies: The Epic Disruption of the Ad Business* (and Everything Else) (London, UK: Penguin Press, 2018).

2. Cowen and Co. Survey quoted by David Lieberman, "'House of Cards' Makes Netflix Subscribers More Loyal: Survey", Deadline.com. Accessed on: 3rd July 2018. https://deadline.com/2013/02/house-of-cards-netflix-subscribers-loyalty-survey-433784/

3. Rae Umsted (Senior Director, Business Development and Content Strategy, Oath Verizon Media Group), interviewed by the author, Los Angeles, November 2017.

4. Yahoo!, *Going There with Anna Gasteyer for Chevrolet Case Study*, 2015.

5.Juniper Research, Ad Fraud: How AI will Rescue Your Budget (London, UK: Juniper Research), 2017.

Chapter 12

1. Animoto, *The Animoto Online and Social Video Marketing Study 2015* (New York, NY: Animoto, 2015).

2. Clifford Chi, "Optimize for the View: The Ideal Length for Your Next Video", Hubspot. Accessed on: 3rd June 2018. https://blog.hubspot.com/marketing/how-long-should-videos-be-on-instagram-twitter-facebook-youtube

Chapter 14

1. Dolly Jones, digital content and strategy director at Condé Nast, speaking at World Forum Disrupt: DigiPublish, 2017

Illustrations and Photos

Chapter 1

Page 36; Illustration 1. *Marketing Storytelling*, with permission, Tom Fishburne, the Marketoonist.com

Page 43; Figure 1. Author's own.

Page 44; Photo 1. *Sergei Eisenstein, 1925*, public domain photograph.

Chapter 2

Page 61; Illustration 2. *Influencer Fatigue*, with permission, Tom Fishburne, the Marketoonist.com.

Page 66; Photo 2. Ludwig von Mises; MisesLibrary.jpg, The Ludwig von Mises Institute.

Chapter 3

Page 75; Illustration 3. *Types of Social Media Strategy*, with permission, Tom Fishburne, the Marketoonist.com.

Page 88; Figure 2. Author's own.

Page 90; Figure 3. Author's own.

Page 94; Figure 4. Author's own.

Chapter 4

Page 108; Figure 5. Jigsaw, *As a fashion brand, we couldn't do what we do without people moving about* #HeartImmigration [Twitter], 11th October 2017. Accessed on: 8th May 2018. https://twitter.com/InsideJigsaw/status/920243167768834048

Page 109; Figure 6. Patagonia, "The President Stole Your Land", Instagram, 2nd December 2017. Accessed on: 3rd May 2018. www.instagram.com/p/BcTKr6Xl6I8/?hl=en

Chapter 6

Page 134; Illustration 4. *Creative Brief*, with permission, Tom Fishburne, the Marketoonist. com.

Page 135; Figure 7. Author's own.

Page 143; Illustration 5. *Viral*, with permission, Tom Fishburne, the Marketoonist.com.

Chapter 7

Page 151; Photo 3 & 4. Prince of Wales – Alan Shawcross, "Prince Charles". Clarence House, London, 2007 and Ozzy Osbourne; Martyn Goodacre, "Ozzy Osbourne at the Langham hotel." London 1997.

Page 152; Photo 4 & 5. Guy Hixon, with permission, Guy "Mr T" Hixon. New York, 2018.

Page 157; Figure 8. Dusty DiMercurio, *The Marketing Funnel Is Dead: Rethinking Content and the Customer Experience*, presentation, ThinkContent, New York, June 2018. Accessed on: 8th May 2018. https://www.slideshare.net/HeatherEng/the-marketing-funnel-is-dead-rethinking-content-and-the-customer-experience-thinkcontent-new-york-2018

Page 159; Figure 9. Ibid

Page 160; Figure 10. Author's own

Chapter 8

Page 164; Figure 11. Author's own.

Page 168; Figure 12. Author's own.

Chapter 10

Page 187; Photo 6. Nilüfer Demir, "KiyiyaVuranInsanlik" ("Humanity Washed Ashore"), September 2015. Doğan News Agency, Bodrum, Turkey.

Page 188; Photo 7. Robert Capa – Magnum Photos, http://www.phaidon.com/agenda/photography/articles/2013/october/23/listen-to-robert-capa-speak/

Chapter 11

Page 199; Illustration 6. *The Tension of Data-Driven Creative*, with permission, Tom Fishburne, the Marketoonist.com.

Chapter 12

Page 204; Figure 13. Ben Ruedlinger, "Does Video Length Matter?", May 2012. Digital Graph, Wistia. Accessed on: 13th February 2018. https://wistia.com/learn/marketing/does-length-matter-it-does-for-video-2k12-edition

Page 207; Figure 14. Author's own.

Page 209; Figure 15. Ooylala, "The Rise of Mobile Video", Ooyala Global Video Index Q1 2018 (San Francisco, CA: Ooyala, 2018).

Chapter 13

Page 218; Figure 16. Author's own.

Page 220; Table 1. Author's own.

Chapter 14

Page 227: Figure 17. Author's own.

Page 228; Illustration 7. *Types of Media*, with permission, Tom Fishburne, the Marketoonist.com.

Page 232; Figure 18. Author's own.

Page 238; Figure 19. Felix Richter, "The State of Live Video Streaming". Statista, Hamburg,

Feb 2017. Accessed on: 5th May 2018 https://www.statista.com/chart/8057/live-video-streaming/.

Page 242; Illustration 8. *Live Streaming Marketing*, with permission, Tom Fishburne, the Marketoonist.com.

Chapter 15

Page 246; Illustration 9. *Marketing Deliverables*, with permission, Tom Fishburne, the Marketoonist.com.

FURTHER READING

Black Box Thinking – Matthew Syed, Hodder and Staughton, 2015

Content Machine: Use Content Marketing to Build a 7-Figure Business with Zero Advertising – Dan Norris, 2015

Contagious: Why Things Catch On – Jonah Berger, Simon & Schuster, 2013

Cultural Strategy: Using Innovative Ideologies to Build Breakthrough Brands – Douglas Holt and Douglas Cameron - Oxford University Press, 2010

Culture's Consequences: Comparing Values, Behaviors, Institutions, and Organizations Across Nations - Geert Hofstede – SAGE Publications, 2001

Do/Purpose – Daniel Hieatt –The Do Book Company, 2014

Enlightenment Now: The Case for Reason, Science, Humanism, and Progress – Daniel Pinker, Viking, 2018

Frenemies: The Epic Disruption of the Advertising Industry (and Everything Else) – Ken Auletta, Penguin Random House, 2018

Grow: How Ideals Power Growth and Profit in the World's Greatest Companies – Jim Stengel – Crown Business, 2011

Hooked: How to Build Habit-Forming Products – Nir Eyal, Portfolio, 2014

How Customers Think: Essential Insights into the Mind of the Market – Gerald Zaltman, Harvard Business School Press, 2003

Into the Woods – John Yorke, The Overlook Press, 2015

Oversubscribed: How to Get People Lining Up to Do Business with You – Daniel Priestley, Capstone, 2015

Path to Purpose: How Young People Find Their Calling in Life - Bill Damon, Simon & Schuster, 2009

Propaganda – Edward Bernays, Ig Publishing, 2004

Positioning: The Battle for Your Mind – Al Ries, and Jack Trout, McGraw-Hill Education, 2001

Seven Habits of Highly Effective People: Powerful Lessons in Personal Change – Stephen R. Covey, Simon & Schuster, 2013

Start with Why – Simon Sinek, Penguin Random House, 2011

Thank You for Being Late: An Optimist's Guide to Thriving in the Age of Accelerations – Thomas L. Friedman, Picador, 2017

The Content Advantage (Clout 2.0): The Science of Succeeding at Digital Business through Effective Content - Colleen Jones, New Riders, 2018

The Naked Corporation: How the Age of Transparency Will Revolutionize Business – Don Tapscott and David Ticoll, Free Press, 2012

The Story Wars: Why Those Who Tell - and Live - the Best Stories Will Rule the Future – Jonah Sachs, Harvard Business Review Press, 2012

This Is Marketing: You Can't Be Seen Until You Learn to See – Seth Godin, Penguin 2018

When: The Scientific Secrets of Perfect Timing – Daniel H. Pink, Riverhead Books, 2018

Zero to One: Notes on Start-ups, or How to Build the Future – Peter Thiel, Random House, 2014

ACKNOWLEDGEMENTS

The literary equivalent of an awards speech rarely makes for particularly gripping reading (especially if you're not in it). One of the most pressing challenges in pulling together a speech or a page is to know where to draw the line. To paraphrase Sir Isaac Newton, if I've seen anything, it's because many people have helped to turn on the lights, the majority of whom are not mentioned here.

A massive and abiding thank you to my business partner, Barnaby Cook, and to Adam Ruddick, Edward Beresford, Lydia Chan, Oliver Atkinson, Guy Hixon and all the amazing people who have made Casual what it is over the years. Building the company has been a thrilling journey, only made possible by the creativity, energy, dedication and friendship of all of you. Building the company has been the most incredible adventure, only made possible by the creativity, energy, dedication and friendship of all of you.

I have learnt so much from the many brilliant clients who we have been able to work with over the years. I have had some of my best days on and off set with you, in many parts of the world. I am grateful to you for the opportunities that your trust has afforded us over the years.

Thanks so much to all the people who agreed to be interviewed and involved in the writing of this book. Their insight was invaluable to my understanding and the formation of my thoughts. This book would be a shadow without them. Chiefly, they are Rory Sutherland at Ogilvy UK, Ana Pedros and Rae Umsted at Oath, Todd Shaiman at Google VR, Hasan Rafiq at EY and Patrick Russell at the BFI. Thanks too for the ongoing friendship and professional guidance of Terry Brissenden, Terry Corby, Mary Keane Dawson, Jo Denye, Adam Etherington, Sami McCabe and Jim Sayer. Thank you to Catalina Schveninger, Oliver Atkinson, Nick Hajdu, Penny Francis for reading and providing feedback on the manuscripts. Thank you to all the people whom I have discussed the concepts in this book with over the years.

Thanks for the ongoing friendship and professional guidance of Terry Brissenden, Terry Corby, Mary Keane Dawson, Jo Denye, Adam Etherington,

Sami McCabe and Jim Sayer. Thank you to Oliver Atkinson, Terry Corby, Penny Francis, Nick Hajdu, Catalina Schveninger, for reading and providing feedback on the manuscripts. Thank you to all the people whom I have discussed the concepts in this book with over the years.

Thank you to Tom Fishburne, the Marketoonist, for allowing me to reproduce his excellent cartoons. They hilariously nail some of the essential truths of the industry. This book would be significantly poorer without them. If you're interested in using any of his work in presentations or your own publications visit his website Marketoonist.com. Thanks to Chris Dudley for turning my sketches into the clear images that appear throughout this book. Thank you to Andy Potts for his stunning cover art. Check him out – he's great – andy-potts. com. This book wouldn't have been possible without the help of Alexa Whitten and her fabulous team at The Book Refinery. She stuck with me throughout the 'messy middle' – the painful middle bit of any creative project when the initial vigour and inspiration is gone, but the end is still nowhere in sight (about six months of this project). As she promised, she got the book out of my head and onto the pages you're reading. This includes Lindsay Corten for her editing and proofreading skills and essential coherence checking. Thanks to Simon Banks of Tallboy Communications and writer of *How to Get Video Right* for the introduction.

I owe a special debt of gratitude to all my family and friends. I grow more grateful for every single relationship I have by the day. Thank you to all of you for making my life the adventure it has been. Thanks to my mum, Penny Francis, for all of the love, understanding and sacrifices that she has made for me and my brother Tim over the years. Thank you to Tim, my brother and erstwhile partner-in-crime, for your friendship, love and support over our many years together. Thank you to Mike Carleton-Smith, the 'Major General', for helping me to strive to be all I can be. Thanks to my late dad, Sir Richard 'Dick' Francis, for the inspiration and opportunity that he gave us all with his boundless energy, ambition and decency. He showed me that it is possible to live a long, successful life in just 58 short years. He has driven me to the best father I can be.

Thank you to my daughter Willow and my niece Grace, who have focused my mind on the future more than any of the personal-development courses or books I've read. Finally, a massive thank you to my wife, Antonia. She has been my rock over the last seven years, pushing me to explore, making me laugh and helping me to be a better person. I promise I won't write another book… for a bit.

ABOUT THE AUTHOR

Nick Francis is a communications consultant, strategist and filmmaker. He co-founded Casual Films in 2006, to cover a 9,000-mile rally to Mongolia in a Mini, following a stint with BBC News. Nick has produced/directed films and animations all over the world, working with hundreds of clients and winning a range of awards in the process. Casual has been voted No.1 corporate production company in the UK for three years running. The company has produced nearly 10,000 films for companies including Adobe, BMW, Facebook, Marriott, PwC, Red Bull and Vodafone among many others. Casual has offices London, New York, Los Angeles and San Francisco (where he now lives with his family). Nick is a Founding Director of the Casual Academy Charity. He is a member of several industry bodies and sits on a number of panels and awards juries. He is a keen snowboarder, cyclist, photographer and cook.

My Purpose

When I was ten years old my father died suddenly. He was a successful, conscientious, inspiring man but he was gone. This was the defining event of the first half of my life. Given 25+ years to think about it, it has affected my approach to life/work in three ways:

1. Life is finite. Enjoy the journey. Don't take yourself too seriously.

2. He still inspires me to work hard to make the things I do the best they can be.

3. Most of what we worry about is inconsequential. Relationships matter, people matter.

I do what I do now because it provides the best way I have found to live these lessons. I work with brands to understand why they do what they do, and then use video – the most powerful communications tool invented – to recruit followers, fans, customers and colleagues.

I'd love to speak to you about how we can do this together.

"Nation shall speak peace unto nation."

- The BBC's motto, inscribed on my dad's gravestone.